CALLING
LAZARUS

By Kaylan James

D1475307

Copyright © 2018 Kaylan James. All rights reserved

Prayers and scripture have been taken from a variety of print and online sources and are believed to be in the public domain.

Cover design by Matthew Scott / JATO Studios

This book is dedicated to my family.
You helped save my life and I'm eternally grateful.

Preface

"The next day, when they came down from the mountain, a large crowd met him. A man in the crowd called out, "Teacher, I beg you to look at my son, for he is my only child. A spirit seizes him and he suddenly screams; it throws him into convulsions so that he foams at the mouth. It scarcely ever leaves him and is destroying him".

–Luke 9:37-3

November 15, 2013

Our three year old, Aiden, raged and screamed as though he was in agonizing pain. He lay on the floor with his back arched, eyes winced shut, fists clinched tightly, shaking and beating the back of his head against the floor as he wailed. It was 11pm and what caused the epic outburst was nothing at all. Or at least nothing we could see. This wasn't his first time. He'd done this many times before and each time, you could see the fright in his eyes

1

as though he was just as scared and confused as we were. Nevertheless, his rage began to trigger my own.

The feeling of dread began to spread throughout our house strangling everything peaceful. Our oldest son, Ryan, paced the floor unsure of what to do, just wishing the noise would stop. He too was getting frustrated more and more by the second and eventually he climbed into his bed and hid beneath his covers to wait out the frantic storm.

My wife, Amanda, cradled Aiden in her arms on the floor and did the only thing she could think to do. In a calm panic she began to recite the Hail Mary over him like her Catholic friends had advised her only days before. About half way through the prayer, Aiden's screams suddenly stopped and he looked up at her, stared her right in the eyes and speaking in a manner that was not his own, calmly said, "You're not scaring me."

An Overview

From 2013 to 2018, my family and I experienced events that can only be described as supernatural. Really, that's putting it lightly. In all honesty, they were nightmarish. Had I not seen them, heard them and, in some cases felt them, I wouldn't have believed them. Not because I didn't believe in them, but because I assumed that the pacts and deals I had made meant my family was untouchable. That was part of the contract. Or so I thought. It took years to fully realize how wrong that assumption was. In the midst of our chaos, I saw the side I had dedicated my life to for so many years, show its true colors. I also saw the side I had sworn to reject, save me along with my family.

In 1989, I turned my back on the Lord and eventually dedicated my life to Satan. I didn't start off Satanic – at least as a label. I didn't wake up one day and decide out of the blue that I'd be a puppet for Lucifer. I began with Wicca soon after transferring from a Christian University in Oklahoma to a University in North Western Pennsylvania. My search for further enlightenment led me to the Hermetic Order of the Golden Dawn then to Enochian and the writings of John Dee and Edward Kelley. I admired the work of Aleister Crowley and my growing admiration for the fallen angels made the step into Satanism as natural as breathing.

I felt at home. I considered myself a soldier and I was proud of the side I chose. I loved and respected Satan in much the same manner that people love and respect God. The feeling of freedom and power I felt blinded me of the tomb I was in. Once I finally began to see the darkness, it took the power of God for me to step out of it and into the sunlight.

We all find ourselves in a dark place. It's where Satan works best. Some places are darker than others. A lot of us become entombed and need help getting out. Some, however, are unwilling to get out. Often times we grow ill in our faith and it becomes a battle. Once our faith is dead, we become servants of Satan. Our relationship with God is disrupted and sometimes even cut off and only through His power can we come back to life. Only He can call us out and free us of our tomb.

A Quick Note About Satanism

I'll talk about Satanism in a general sense and even the feelings I had while following it. However, I won't go into too much detail about how I found Satan's path nor will I go into lengthy discussions about the rituals I performed and took place in. My journey out of the evil one's grasp should shed enough light on how scary that path really is. Plus, I don't want to glorify him by making that life seem wonderful. There is enough temptation in the world as it is. This train is on a one-way trip out of Satan Central Station and there's plenty of room for you, and me and everyone we know.

As I write this, I'm still on my journey. A journey I never thought I'd take and one that I'm now convinced is meant to never end. As the healed man said to the Pharisees in John 9:25, *"There is one thing I do know: I was blind, but now I see!"* I want to see as much as I can. I want to feel God's love in my heart and radiate that outward in my daily life. I was blind and prideful and thought I held the power over my life but the power of God is much greater than my own, and that lesson didn't come easy. There's a saying by Joyce Meyer that goes, "I may not be where I want to be, but thank God I'm not where I used to be." To that I say a resounding AMEN!

So they rolled the stone aside. Then Jesus looked up to heaven and said, "Father, thank you for hearing me. You always hear me, but I said it out loud for the sake of all these people standing here, so that they will believe You sent me." Then Jesus shouted, "Lazarus, come out!" And the dead man came out, his hands and feet bound in grave

clothes, his face wrapped in a head cloth. Jesus told them,
"Unwrap him and let him go!" – John 11:41-44

1

Satan's Soldier

Next the devil took Him to the peak of a very high mountain and showed Him all the kingdoms of the world and their glory. "I will give it all to You," he said, "if You will kneel down and worship me." – Matthew 4:8-9

My Wiccan name was Jael. The name came to me and wouldn't let me go. I tried to think of others but that one in particular sat there in the front of my mind and refused to budge. It just nagged and nagged at me until I gave in and used it. We'll actually circle back around to that later. Just remember that name.

Since a Shaman taught me, I had an animal spirit guide as well. I instantly chose a bear without a second thought. Actually at the time I felt the bear chose me. He was like my guardian angel in both the dream world and material world. I felt protected and watched over and often wished I'd have an encounter with a real bear so I could soak up its essence even if it killed me. I thought I'd receive the bear's spiritual energy if one attacked me. I wished for that. I'll admit a lot of things in this book. I'm not proud of them.

I charged pentacles by the full moon. I often wrote in runes and knew the alphabets of several magickal languages. I walked through forests soaking up the life energy that saturated every rock, leaf and branch. I meditated in incense filled rooms to connect with the forces that permeated the very walls and all my senses. And while I felt free and deeply in tune with nature, I felt something was missing. I needed more. So I went looking for more in much darker places. What I found changed me slowly and deliberately over the course of 20 years. What I found was Satan.

Being a Satanist is remarkably easy. I dare say it's almost lazy, at least in a spiritual sense. Becoming a Satanist is even easier. Just focus entirely on yourself. There's really nothing to it. There aren't any lengthy questionnaires or applications to fill out. Just defy God. We fall into it all the time and most of us dabble in Satanism everyday; we just don't recognize it for what it is. I know people will scoff at that idea but to them I ask, where exactly do you think your sin comes from? How about your pride, selfishness, hatred, gluttony, and lust just to mention a few? If you can willingly ignore God then you possess the essential building blocks of Satanism. It's that easy. It's easy to follow Satan. It takes work to follow God.

To make matters worse, Satan makes it extremely simple to join. Especially now thanks to the internet, you can instantly get all sorts of information and contacts and things I didn't have access to when I started out. Even the media that we're bombarded with every day pushes us further away from God. You don't even have to be overflowing with spiritual doubt to be eligible for Satanism. If you have the tiniest sliver of doubt, even if it's barely detectable, Satan can work with it. Everyone is welcome and it's tailor-made to fit your desires. Bring a friend. They're welcome too.

Satan is a master at marketing. The Nike guys and Bud Light guys and the creators of all those amazing Super Bowl commercials, they're amateurs compared to what Satan can do. He can package eternal death and torment and sell it like a free all-inclusive Disney vacation. And he'll have people literally killing each other to get it. Satan targets the young. Even children aren't safe. There aren't any off limits rules to this battle. In 1997, the R.J Reynolds Tobacco Company finally and reluctantly ended the "Joe Camel" ad campaigns after a lawsuit was brought against the company in 1991. The lawsuit stated that the company was knowingly and systematically targeting children and young people with their cool and trendy Disneyesque Joe Camel ads that first began in the US in 1988. The suit further alleged that underage smoking accounted for $476 million of Camel cigarette sales in 1992 and compared that to the mere $6 million when the campaign started in 1988. Unfortunately, Satan can't be sued. He targets children. He targets the young. The more impressionable they are, the better. It's a shrewd game and the stakes are high.

Satanists don't worship Satan like Christians worship God. That's a common misconception. They may admire Satan or even love him, but Satanists worship them selves. Satanism is a very self centered path and you alone are the master of your life and destiny. Whatever happens to you either good or bad is because you alone made that happen. No matter if you're a successful billionaire or starving and homeless, it was your decisions and actions that put you there, period. And it will be your decisions and actions that will change that status. Not God, you.

The self-indulging perks state that the material and lustful pleasures of the world are yours for the taking because after all, you're just another animal and why would you have desires, especially primal ones, and deny them? It's empowering in its selfishness and you feel somewhat godlike. The freedom I felt was an illusion and I was too focused on the worldly pleasures to notice the chain around my neck. I did what I wanted when I wanted regardless of whom it hurt and the demons I followed pushed me on. I loved them for it.

I had a sensation that I could actually look "behind the curtain" and see all the hypocrisy that the church of God had to offer with remarkable clarity. I felt I had eaten the forbidden fruit offered by Satan in the Garden of Eden but rather than being ashamed, I wanted more. I wanted lots more to the point that I gorged myself on it.

I loved my life. I loved my demonic team. I actually looked forward to Hell because I was convinced that the spooky images of the lake of fire and eternal torment with the wailing and gnashing of teeth were all a big lie spread by the followers of God to ensure more money into their collection plates. I often used to joke that the parties in Hell would be a lot more fun. I can go on and on. I'm fortunate that I can shake my head now at my staggering naivety.

It's hard for some to imagine, but I was a proud Satanist. I believed whole-heartedly that the angel I came to love was courageous for taking on God, head-on; who's brainwashed followers were the masterminds of a crooked establishment. It's amazing what you can convince yourself as being true and even more amazing what you'll defend. But I was proud of my path. I prided myself on being the "real thing" in much the same manner someone would claim to be a true Broncos fan or a true Star Wars fan. I didn't walk around with a Baphomet t-shirt, flashing devil-horn hand gestures and making myself a spectacle for the sake of shock value. I hated people like that. My pride made me arrogant and hateful not only toward those that followed God but at times to other Satanists as well.

In the early days of social media, I actively set out to harm or destroy faiths whenever the opportunity presented itself. I roamed the AOL chat rooms (remember those?) looking for faiths to damage. For those that aren't familiar with AOL chat rooms, America Online, or more commonly known as AOL, was a social media pioneer. They helped lead the way and most everyone was using it. When you logged onto your AOL account, you could browse the Internet, check your AOL mail or visit one of hundreds of member created "chat rooms" which were filled with people talking about everything from Tex-Mex recipes to RP gaming to biblical topics depending on the title of each chat room. The topics seemed endless. If you couldn't find one you liked, you could just start up your own and people would wander in. It was the Christian ones that I targeted most. Like a lion singling out the weakest antelope, I looked for the weakest in their faith and went after them unmercifully. Sometimes I encountered people strong in their faith, other times not. Decades later and a tour through RCIA would reveal that what I was doing was in fact breaking the fifth commandment; "Thou shalt not kill." That commandment isn't limited to murder of the flesh. It also means murder of the spirit. I was an assassin of faith and I found pleasure in it. As I write this, it's hard not to dwell on the guilt. I can only hope that those I attacked had better faith than I gave them credit for.

I made pacts with spirits and demons using blood signatures. Other bodily fluid could have been used but I settled on blood. It felt more personal. I didn't see it as selling my soul. That's a common misconception even though ironically, that's what I was really doing. But it wasn't like going down to the crossroads at midnight and trading my soul for fame. The pacts were more like partnerships. They were agreements or contracts with certain spirits and demons to obtain certain goals with both sides working until that goal is met. The idea of selling your soul to Satan and instantly getting rich is more in line with fairy tales and Hollywood. Likewise, the idea of working with demons like you're hiring contractors to help you renovate your bathroom and then assuming they'll leave when the job is done is more in line with ignorance. We assume we actually have the power to ask or even tell demons what to do. They don't really work for you. They aren't for hire.

I made my blood oath allegiance to Satan and denounced God. It wasn't gory like one would imagine. I cut my hand and signed with the blood. I felt good about it. My hand hurt but I felt free and felt I was on my way to greatness. I had three particular demons that I admired and felt close to. There is power in names, so therefore I won't be giving them the satisfaction here by revealing them. But at the time, I felt embraced and respected. I looked at the demons as family. That might be an odd way to think about it. I felt that they watched over me and protected me and that not only was I needed but respected as well. I wasn't scared of Hell. I was gunning for a management position when I got there.

It would take me years to finally learn that demons didn't need any friends nor did they seek any out. I would like to say that I was just collateral damage in the great spiritual war but I know in my heart that isn't true. Despite my years of dedication, they hated me. Loathed would be a more fitting word. I meant nothing to them and would always be nothing. The "family" I'd grown to love only wanted one thing. They wanted to destroy me, and let God watch as my soul was torn apart at the seams.

In some aspects, I was a Luciferian. In others I was a Satanist. The label doesn't matter because Satan doesn't care about your label. Try not to get hung up on them. A lot of people call themselves "spiritual but not religious" – whatever that means. It's a good option, I guess, to make you feel like you're in the game but without the hassle of commitment. Call yourself whatever you want. Call yourself an Atheist if that makes you feel better. As long as you're not following God then Satan is happy. I'll break it down like this, and on the surface, it's very simple. There are only two teams out there, God's team and Satan's team. If you're not playing for one, you're playing for the other regardless of the label you're comfortable with.

Think of it this way, Satanism is your default state. The ease and convenience of living how you want without putting God first is intriguing and most of us tend to take the easy road. To some degree, we do it daily. Normally, many of us don't even think about pushing God aside to get what we want or act how we want. We just do it and if we are aware of it, we use the "I'm only human" excuse. We live in the now. We want instant results and we'll generally take them whether we know or not if Satan is the one providing them. Your heart is never empty. You're either busy filling it with God, or you're busy filling it with Satan. I'll give you a minute to absorb all that.

2

A Boy And His Bear

Keep watch over yourselves and all the flock of which the Holy Spirit has made you overseers. Be shepherds of the church of God, which He bought with his own blood. I know that after I leave, savage wolves will come in among you and will not spare the flock. Even from your own number, men will arise and distort the truth in order to draw away disciples after them. –Acts 20: 28-30

According to the James family legend, I Kaylan James, in 1976 at the age of 6, was solely responsible for bringing my grandfather back to church. His name was Mike, which oddly enough wasn't even his real name. It was actually Horace. As fate would have it, an old employer told him his name was terrible and started calling him "Mike" and there it stayed from then on. We all just called him Papa Bear, or just Bear for short.

Growing up I had always known Bear to never miss a single Sunday service. As I got older I learned that wasn't always true. He had fallen away citing things like hypocrisy and anything else he could use to justify his avoidance of church. My Granny was a rock in her faith and she kept going without him, praying for him every Sunday.

As the story goes, one Sunday evening my parents and I were at their house to pick Granny up for church service. Bear was sitting on the back patio and I went out to be with him. As we sat there together, I asked him if he was coming with us. He said no but that he'd see us after it was over. I then looked at him and said, "If you're staying then I'm staying. And if you're going to Hell then I'm coming with you."

With that, Bear got up from his chair and went inside the house and started changing his clothes to get ready for church at the amazement and delight of my Granny. After that, he never again missed a single Sunday church service. Now of course being older and hopefully wiser, I know now that it was in fact God's plan working through the innocence of a 6 year old but the family story remains to this day nonetheless.

Standing at only 5'4", Bear was bigger than life. I grew up with stories about him that made me want to be him. He was a notorious scrapper. His nose was crooked from fighting in his early years. He helped put a cow into a second floor hotel room in Cheyenne, Oklahoma. Under threat of being kicked out of school, he walked out on his own never to return then traded a guitar for a horse. Those two stories always shared the same sentence. I'm sure there was more to it but that's how the legend has been passed down. Later in life he had a cast mending his broken arm. The cast bothered him while he drove so he pulled over, took out his pocketknife, cut the cast off and tossed it out the window. Bear did what he wanted and as I grew up, I watched him in awe. He was like a pirate. He was my super hero.

The story that stuck with me that made me wonder if he truly had powers that dipped into the super natural or if he was truly just a badass, was when he acquired his German Shepard that he named Chula. In the spring of 1972, a van pulled up to the café Bear owned in Taos, NM. In his lifetime, Bear owned several successful businesses despite his short-lived education. The café in Taos was just one. Inside the van were several hippies and a

German Shepard they were scared the death of. It was during the hippie movement – rainbow colored everything, macramé, lava lamps, VW microbuses and "Make love not war", far out, man. I never knew how they all ended up in the same van with a dog they didn't get along with, as it was never part of the story. At any rate, Bear walked over to the van and could clearly see how frightened the occupants were of this dog. The dog looked at Bear and growled at him just as he had done to the others. With that, Bear popped him on the snout with his hand and stared the dog down. Immediately all those present, including the dog, knew who the alpha really was. Bear took the dog from the van, claimed him as his and named him Chula. The hippies drove away, less one dog and all were happier for it.

Bear and I were very close. It wasn't a secret that I was the favorite. But then again, I was the only grandson. I was spoiled. I got everything. And while I was the favorite of his, he was the favorite of mine. We couldn't have been any closer and I often feel that a part of me died with him. In my eyes, he could do no wrong.

It was because of him that I got baptized at thirteen years old. Not because of anything he taught me about

God, but because they were in town visiting and I wanted to make him proud as he and my Granny sat with us at church one Sunday morning. When it was done, my father took me aside with my hair still dripping wet and said he was proud as well and added that the spiritual road wasn't always going to be easy. His wisdom went way over my head and I had no idea what he was talking about but nodded like I did.

Bear was a Freemason. I remember clearly growing up, always seeing a certain ring that he wore. It was big, gold with a silver double-headed eagle and a diamond in the center with the number 32 in a little triangle. I remember the badges on his car of the square and compass as well as the Shriner's scimitars. I remember seeing his fez hat and thinking it looked funny. I grew up with these things and to me they were the symbols of my favorite relative and I wanted to be part of that too. Later when he died, I received his level-14 Masonic ring. I wore it proudly for years. I probably shouldn't have for several reasons but I did because I loved him. I knew nothing about the ring itself other than it was his and it was Masonic. To me, that was enough and I admired the Masons because of him.

Plenty can be said about the Masons, both their contributions as well as their controversies. I'm no expert on the Masons. I haven't spent my life studying them nor have I been one. Anything I say about them should be taken with that fact in mind. What I know and am an expert of is that I loved my grandfather and because of that, I too wanted to be a Mason like he was. I'm here to neither promote nor slander nor dive too deeply into this topic.

I've heard by some, that the Masons are steeped in Satanism, which only the highest ranks are aware of and participate in. I've also heard the exact opposite from former members who are now practicing Catholics. Bear was at least 32-level and I can't imagine him ever participating in any satanic ritual whether aware or unaware. But then my opinion is extremely biased. He was a wonderful man and I'll go to my grave believing so. But be that as it may, the question remains. Are they in fact clouded in Satanism? Is it so well hidden that even the members themselves below 33rd level don't even see it?

In the Masonic literature of Eliphas Levi's "Mysteries of Magic", he states, *"What is more absurd and more impious than to attribute the name of Lucifer to the devil, that is, to personified evil? The intellectual Lucifer is the spirit of intelligence and love; it is the Paraclete, it is the Holy Spirit, while the physical Lucifer is the great agent of universal magnetism."*

There is a lot of secrecy surrounding the Masons and the "blood oaths" attached to breaking that silence. Whether symbolic or not, the idea of promising such an oath is heavily frowned upon by the Catholic Church. They go on record saying you cannot be both a Mason and a Catholic. Pick one. I will quote Catholic.com on the subject of Freemasonry as they explain the stance of the Catholic Church very plainly.

"Freemasonry is incompatible with the Catholic faith. Freemasonry teaches a naturalistic religion that espouses indifferentism, the position that a person can be equally pleasing to God while remaining in any religion.

Masonry is a parallel religion to Christianity. The New Catholic Encyclopedia states, 'Freemasonry displays all the elements of religion, and as such it becomes a rival to the religion of the Gospel. It

includes temples and altars, prayers, a moral code,
worship, vestments, feast days, the promise of
reward or punishment in the afterlife, a hierarchy,
and initiation and burial rites.'

Masonry is also a secret society. Its initiates
subscribe to secret blood oaths that are contrary to
Christian morals. The prospective Mason swears
that if he ever reveals the secrets of Masonry -
secrets which are trivial and already well-known -
he wills to be subject to self-mutilation or to
gruesome execution. (Most Masons, admittedly,
never would dream of carrying out these
punishments on themselves or on an errant
member).

Historically, one of Masonry's primary objectives has
been the destruction of the Catholic Church; this is
especially true of Freemasonry as it has existed in
certain European countries. In the United States,
Freemasonry is often little more than a social club,
but it still espouses a naturalistic religion that
contradicts orthodox Christianity."

It would be nice to talk to Bear right now and ask him about everything concerning the Masons and whether or not he knew of or participated in any occult oriented rituals. If the accusation had any truth to it, he'd sit down and tell me all about it. If not, he'd sock me one for the insult. We hear of the good works done by the Freemasons and the Shriners but that doesn't necessarily mean the organizations are automatically good. The notorious drug lord Pablo Escobar, was known by many to be wonderfully generous. That doesn't mean he was always good either. As it turned out, in the end my hopes of ever becoming a Mason to honor the memory of the late great Papa Bear eventually ended with significant spiritual resistance as I renounced the Masons based on possible ancestral ties to me, brought about knowingly or unknowingly. We'll talk more about my renouncing later.

3

Plans

Satan, who is the god of this world, has blinded the minds of those who don't believe. They are unable to see the glorious light of the Good News. They don't understand this message about the glory of Christ, who is the exact likeness of God. –2 Corinthians 4:4

God has a plan. He always, always has a plan. It may not happen on our preferred schedule or by our preferred method. We sometimes don't even see his plan reveal it self until days, months or even years later. Lazarus's sisters, Mary and Martha, who all three were friends of Jesus, sent word to him in John 11:3 that their brother was gravely ill and needed assistance. Even then God was at work. Mary and Martha expected Jesus to drop everything and come immediately. But Jesus states in verse 4, *"Lazarus's sickness will not end in death. No, it happened for the glory of God so that the Son of God will receive glory from this."* He needed them to have faith as well as patience; the same that he asks of us.

We all want God to show himself. We all want signs to prove his existence. We all want the burning bush and the deep James Earl Jones voice booming over the clouds. We tend to need some sort of tangibility to move our faith forward. It would be nice if he just sent angels to tell us exactly what to do like he did in the scriptures. But who says he doesn't still do that? We're talking about the creator of life, supernovas, and microscopic atoms unseen by the naked eye and giant stars that dwarf our sun. Surely he can reach you whether it's through your neighbor, your sister, your 6-year old grandson sitting with you on your patio or even your wife. God sends you angels. God always has a plan. As the saying goes, if you want to make God laugh, tell him YOUR plans. My plan was not to ever set foot inside a church again. Things didn't work out that way. God sent Amanda.

I met Amanda on November 7, 2005 through an online dating site. A few months prior, my eleven-year marriage to my previous wife was declared officially over by the state of Oklahoma and I was officially on the market. Amanda wasn't religious by any means and I conveniently left my Satan status off my Match.com profile. After all, my spiritual life was supposed to stay under wraps until I decided to change that or not – My life, my plans.

As it turned out, we hit it off immediately. So well in fact that just a month after we met, she moved from a town she'd lived in her entire life to move with me a hundred miles away into a horrible little house that we rented that we nicknamed "The Swiss-Cheese House." There were so many holes in that place. The front door didn't fully reach the floor and had a space wide enough for the Oklahoma red dirt to blow in. Really it should have been condemned before we were ever allowed to move into it. We could hear squirrels running around chasing each other in the attic at night. It was awful. Obviously both of our families thought we were crazy. But that's love for you. Besides, love and crazy tend to look the same.

During this time and for a long time after, I never shared my satanic pact because honestly, I didn't think it was anyone's business. Nor did I think it would ever cause an issue. What people don't know won't hurt them, right? No harm no foul. Not to mention, I never would have thought in a million years that Amanda would find God. I had planned to keep my satanic secret buried. I thought it was a pretty watertight plan.

We were married a relatively short time after in August 2006, and in June 2007, Ryan was born. We really didn't waste much time. To my surprise, Amanda suggested that maybe we start going to church as a way to bring up our children with some sort of morals. The suggestion hung in the air, dripping with unease and stank with my deepest loathing but I somehow kept on a smile and went along with the idea thinking she wouldn't really stick with it. Besides, if she was happy then I'd be happy and I knew it wouldn't take long for her to feel overwhelmed and drift away from it. In the meantime I'd help to influence her away making her think it was her idea. I wasn't worried.

By this time, I wasn't an outwardly practicing Satanist making the secret easier to keep. Come to think of it, I was always that way. You had to look hard and get into some deep conversations with me to even pick up on it. Even then, unless you knew what you were looking for, chances were good that you'd miss it anyway. I wasn't in it for the shock value.

Any time someone mentions Satanism, people instantly get Hollywood images of black candles, black fingernails and giant pentagrams drawn on the floor where the carpet used to be with some sort of deceased animal in the middle. It wasn't like that, nor was it ever. I didn't dress like you'd imagine a Satanist to dress. We have this idea in our minds about what they're supposed to look like in the same way we assume what angels or rock stars or plumbers are supposed to look like. I just looked normal. Most Satanists do.

In 2008, we found a local Protestant church and started attending. I had avoided churches for years, refusing to step foot inside one. I remember being surprised that I didn't go into convulsions and burst into flames when I stepped through the door on our first Sunday. I pigeonholed God as being like a mean drunk. Betting on the life of Job and tormenting Abraham by making him think he had to kill his own son. I didn't appreciate those stories and missed the point completely other than seeing them at face value. But I wasn't on fire, so maybe I snuck in under the radar. I

I was raised a Protestant. I wasn't a stranger to church. I believed in it. I just wasn't thrilled to be there. I was a Satanist not an Atheist. Even the Devil believes in God. We read in a letter from James to the scattered Christians of the nations, *"You say you have faith, for you believe that there is one God. Good for you! Even the demons believe this, and they tremble in terror."* –James 2:19

Amanda, however, was a stranger in a strange land and didn't know a single Bible story. But this church idea was for her and our family and seeing that my skin didn't catch fire like I assumed it would, all seemed fine and I went along with it. In fact, I went along with it for 2 years and we tried our best to fit in. Amanda was always frustrated and couldn't grasp it all and I didn't know how nor did I want to really explain the Bible to her. I think my unwillingness to do it made me think I didn't know how. Either way, I was only there for show.

God was working on me then and even though I "played church" really well, my heart was still rooted with Satan. I was the house built on sand. My foundation was cracked, and mostly missing but my curtains looked great! My heart hadn't changed and God knew it all along. I'm embarrassed even now to admit that I was trying to fool God. I had everyone else fooled but he knew I was going to do that before I ever did it. Lucky for me, God isn't one to shy away from tearing something down to rebuild it better.

Our youngest son Aiden, was born in July 2010 and by November, Amanda and I had plummeted into a very dark place spiritually, and emotionally. We'd already spent a solid year battling autism with our oldest and felt crushed when Aiden was born with a cleft lip and open palate. God was kicking us while we were down. Or, that's what we believed anyway. We had certain things on our list that we were sure we were getting punished for. We assumed God had a Karma style approach to dishing out consequences. So while it wasn't a huge surprise for us that we were going through hard times via God's wrath, it upset us that our children were the ones being made to take on most of the suffering.

The challenges we faced were daunting enough without the added stress of Aiden's issues. Granted, we knew none of them were his fault but the constant feeding struggles brought on by the cleft lip and open pallet combined with his inability to sleep well, were very unforgiving on our already taxed mentalities. I was angry and dropped the idea of following God, even for pretend, for the last time. Amanda was in my boat and she too, hated God for what he did to us. Even now she'll admit that she would get physically sick when anyone would say they would pray for us. I felt that this was a good time to shift gears.

She knew I had been Wiccan but that was it. My plan was to bring her in slowly much like the path I took. The "Vanilla Road" is much easier and less scary. You never lead with the Satan card unless they bring it up first. So I bought her a few Wiccan books to get her started and was delighted in the idea of she and I being on the same page. It felt wonderful. We both hated God. We wanted nothing to do with God or anyone that had anything to do with him. We were angry and felt rejected and while Amanda felt she had wasted those years going to church, it was just confirmation for me that Satanism was where my home really was. Even if she and the kids just stayed Wiccan, that was fine by me. I wouldn't have taken the kids further until they were older anyway. Life was good. A couple years went by and we maintained our "God free" status. Then Aiden started seeing monsters.

4

Monsters, Monica, And Father Ray

When the seventy-two disciples returned, they joyfully reported to Him, "Lord, even the demons obey us when we use Your name!"

"Yes", he told them, "I saw Satan fall from heaven like lightning! Look, I have given you authority over all the power of the enemy, and you can walk among snakes and scorpions and crush them. Nothing will injure you."

–Luke 10:17-19

Much of my journey out of Satanism began with Aiden. At only three years old, he had an interesting gift. He could see demons. Of course if you asked him, he probably wouldn't refer to it as a "gift". It wasn't something he was ever happy about. We didn't know of course that what he was seeing were demons. He said he saw monsters. I think most kids see monsters at some point. Naturally as parents we just brushed it off as typical child behavior. Kids see monsters. He'll grow out of it. Easiest parenting problem ever. Parent of the Year Award goes to...

Demons weren't exactly on our mind. Besides why would demons be messing with my kids? I was part of Satan's team. My family was off limits. Right? That's how it should work. But as time went on, he would see them more frequently and not just during the night. He'd see them in our house, during the day. He'd sit on his bed and point them out. He'd point them out in the kitchen if they were around. They weren't always scary and we weren't overly concerned. We'd joke with him and ask him if they're hungry and maybe we should make them a sandwich. Our worry level was at zero.

Our concern really didn't take a turn until Aiden started waking up at 3:30am every night. Not 3:29 or 3:31, but precisely 3:30. Ryan could sleep through a beginner's kazoo band practice. But Aiden was always up, startled by something. It wouldn't have even been noticed if it were a one-time thing. It became a nightly ritual. We could actually have set our clocks to it. Amanda mentioned this to several friends, most of whom just brushed it off. But her Catholic friends however, didn't brush it off. They had concerns and started asking questions – lots of questions. First monsters and now 3:30am wake ups? They didn't like that one bit.

As a Satanist, there were things I wouldn't tolerate. I'm sure you can guess many of them. At the top of the list was prayer. Followed immediately by anyone praying for my soul. Nothing disgusted me more. To my surprise, Catholicism in particular also ranked at the top of the list. I already knew I wasn't a fan but my demons despised it. I felt them. I felt their hatred and it burned in my gut and swelled through my body in a rage unlike any other. I didn't know about this unparalleled hatred until Monica started talking to Amanda about spirituality. Needless to say, Monica is one of those Catholic friends. And while she and her husband are now the Godparents of our children and we adore their family, there was a time that I hated her and wanted her a million miles away from my wife.

It started out innocently enough. But then again, it only takes a spark to burn down a forest. I could tell immediately upon entering the room if Amanda was on the phone with Monica. I could feel it. A thousand voices would ring in my head and my insides would recoil. I wouldn't even have to hear the conversation. I just knew.

My blood boiled. My transformation was instant and my normal mild laid-back self was replaced with anger. My loathing was evident and it confused Amanda as to where it was all coming from.

I couldn't tell her. I wouldn't tell her. How do you tell your wife that she unknowingly married a Satanist? That's not an easy conversation to approach from any angle. I stayed quiet about its true origin and played the Protestant versus Catholic card. My perfect plan was unraveling the more she talked to Monica and I knew I'd lose my wife to God. I could feel it. I hated that. My demons hated that and I had many of them. Our house was combative and while Amanda was in the dark about me, I think Monica had a good idea and rather than step down, she stepped up. I hated her for that.

Monica was armed with God and her weapons were sharp and her armor was thick. My many demons knew this long before I did. They hated her talking to my wife because they knew the wrench she could throw into my perfect plan was a powerful wrench. It always amazes me when I think back on it just how many Catholics ran toward us when they recognized the spiritual warfare we were struggling with. They seemed eager for it and reveled in the battle. Monica was one of those. She was a true soldier of God. She was the Professor X to my Magneto...the Luke to my Vader. For you *Die Hard* fans, she was the John McClane in my Nakatomi Plaza! Do you get what I'm saying? She was wrecking my lair! She was knowledgeable and insightful and to me that spelled trouble. I was beside myself in anger and fear thinking it couldn't possibly get any worse.

Then Jennifer came into the picture: yet another Catholic friend with concerns. There seemed to be no shortage of Catholic friends. She approached Amanda and told her she had some Holy water to put on the kids. Amanda rolled her eyes at this gesture but still planned to go to her house and pick it up with the mind set that she'd do it just to rule it out. Even with Monica in her ear, Amanda still wasn't on board. That wasn't enough to deter her friends. God kept sending them.

While all this was going on, I had taken a new job that had me traveling frequently to Chicago. The monster sightings always ramped up when I was out of town. I had finally returned home shortly before Amanda received the Holy water from her friend. Since I was the head of the household, she said I should be the one to apply it. I wasn't spiritually qualified to even attempt such a thing but I thought it was a bunch of nonsense anyway and didn't think much about it. When nothing changed, I could at least say I used the magic water on my kid. Done and done. Next.

Reiki

The day Amanda went to pick up the Holy water, she had a Reiki session that just happened to be nearby. She was very much into New Age healing and actually had plans to take classes to become a Reiki master. For those of you that aren't familiar with Reiki, I'll explain it some and why it's significant to the story. As a side note, just like the Masons, I'm neither promoting nor slandering the practice. Only reporting what happened. While the Catholic Church publically and specifically denounces the use of Reiki, you have the freedom to decide for yourself if it's good, bad or indifferent.

According to Reiki.org, it's described as, "...*a Japanese technique for stress reduction and relaxation that also promotes healing. It is administered by "laying on hands" and is based on the idea that an unseen "life force energy" flows through us and is what causes us to be alive.*

If one's "life force energy" is low, then we are more likely to get sick or feel stress, and if it is high, we are more capable of being happy and healthy."

Amanda went to a lady's house for the session and was led to an upstairs room where she laid down on a table and the woman put her into a trance. While under the trance, she started seeing things flash by in her mind. Images of violent, bloody graphic scenes of murder and demonic chaos flew into her thoughts. Her whole body vibrated at first and it grew into a full tremor, which shook the very table she laid on. While she felt and even thought the entire session lasted only a few minutes, it had in fact gone a whole hour.

She came home visibly shaken and disturbed by the things she saw while she was under the trance. Her once excited drive to learn Reiki and be a master with the ability to treat others with it, was diminished significantly and she didn't quite know what to make of it. She didn't know where the images came from and their level of gore and violence troubled her greatly.

That night I applied the Holy water to Aiden before bed. I wet my finger with it and made the sign of the cross on his forehead asking God to bless him and protect him. I didn't even think to put it on Ryan so he went to bed without it. Amanda went to bed as well and I went downstairs to get a project done that had a tight deadline. Sure enough, at exactly 3:30, Amanda was awakened by footsteps running into our room. However, it wasn't Aiden. It was Ryan.

She let him crawl into bed with her and as he lay with his back to her she heard him talking about scary sounds coming from the upstairs hall bathroom. Now it's normal for us, when I'm up late, to leave on a light over our master bathroom shower that spills a little of that light into our room. So you can see but it's not overly bright. She turned Ryan over and saw that his eyes were all black and "swimming" much in the same manner as oil sits on top of water. Then she noticed in horror that he had blood streaming from both nostrils all down his face. He was covered in it. She jumped up and went and got me. We cleaned him up and he was clearly shaken. At that moment, Amanda was convinced that the spiritual warfare Monica spoke of was very much real. Both Amanda and Ryan stayed awake the rest of the night while Aiden, who had been blessed with Holy water, slept peacefully. Furthermore, Amanda's plans to become a Reiki master were forever gone.

Shock and Awe

The next morning I agreed to have a priest come visit the house. I agreed more out of anger that "rogue demons" were messing with my family. I was still under the illusion that I was off limits. It wasn't supposed to be this way! I was a soldier of Satan dammit! I had tenure! I didn't have an employee handbook to consult and Hell isn't big with HR. I was irritated and confused. So I agreed to the plan of the priest. What I didn't know, was that this was no ordinary dime a dozen priest – in my mind, they were all the same. Amanda had scheduled an exorcist employed by the Archdiocese and one of only a handful in the country. I've always heard that during times of war, the military would often times begin a campaign with a 'Shock and Awe" tactic to throw their adversaries off kilt. Having Father Ray visit the house was every bit a shock and awe tactic.

By the time Father Ray arrived, I was already regretting my decision. That regret spiked when he stepped into my home. My demons surely knew him. My thoughts were scattered and all I could focus on was that my lair was being invaded and the invader was unwelcome. Anytime Amanda recounts the visit, she always talks about how angry, boastful and arrogant I was. How I didn't even look or sound like myself. Even my mannerisms had changed. My demons didn't want Father Ray there. To make things worse, he didn't travel alone. He walked into the house with a team of 3 others who frequently accompanied him during his visits. Two of which were very knowledgeable about many facets of the occult world, with one of them being particularly sensitive to spiritual presence. Years later she recounted that our house was ripe with dark spirits. The third of the trio of team members was a very knowledgeable gentleman who was employed by the Archdiocese of Kansas City. At first meeting, I despised them all. Shock and awe had begun. Amanda pulled out the big guns. I remember that I loved her, but I didn't particularly like her that day.

He moved through the house commenting on things he didn't like such as the lamps we had that bore a likeness to Eastern Religion. Having been a fantasy artist for many years, I had paintings up on the walls of artists in the genre that I admired and followed. Father Ray didn't like those either. In fact, most of the things in my art studio weren't well received by the intrusive priest. My last straw snapped when he pointed at 2 large Native American Kachina dolls I had on a shelf. The same Kachina dolls my grandfather once owned and the ones I admired as a kid growing up hoping and dreaming to one day finally have. Father Ray didn't like them and suggested they should go since they could be a possible demonic gateway. My tolerance for the priest in my lair was gone and my unhappiness for this unwanted intrusion was evident. But God was in charge and things were about to get a lot crazier.

The one part of the Father Ray visit that I remember clear as a bell, was when he stood at the kitchen table and began to put on his vestments. I watched him. I burned holes through him. I hoped he could feel it. I wanted him to hurt but he seemed unfazed.

He then opened his Bible and began reading in Latin as he blessed the house. More shock and awe. I don't know if any of you have ever been mean enough to pour salt on a slug or burn ants with a magnifying glass. If you have, or can imagine it, you'll get the idea of how I instantly felt. Inside my head, screamed a thousand voices all hissing over and over the same word, "LIES!" I couldn't focus on anything. The room spun around me. I held on to the counter. My senses were completely out of whack and all I could think to do was put my hands over my ears to stop the noise crashing down on me, which threw me completely off balance as though I was suddenly struck with vertigo. I hated him. I thought horrible things – terrible, evil, violent things. I wanted to hit him with something but I couldn't move. I wanted him dead. I remember that part startling me. I couldn't stop thinking it. I couldn't stop the relentless screaming in my head. And while all this was going on, Aiden wasn't fairing well either.

Aiden was and still is very sensitive to the demons I had allowed into our home. His reaction to the priest and his team in our house closely resembled mine. He acted out, purposefully and methodically, drawing attention and hampering the process as well as a three-year-old could. But the prayers didn't stop. The blessings didn't stop. The four invaders in my home marched forward and laid waste to my sense of security in the lair I had worked hard to build and I could feel the seething disgust in the demons that surrounded me.

5

Gateways

With the Lord's authority I say this: Live no longer as the Gentiles do, for they are hopelessly confused. Their minds are full of darkness; they wander far from the life God gives because they have closed their minds and hardened their hearts against him. –Ephesians 4:17-18

A lot can be said about gateways. Father Ray pointed out many possible ones, most of which were in my studio where I spent the majority of my time. But what are they? Are they always physical in nature? A lot of us instantly conjure up images of a mysterious well-sized hole in the basement with an eerie green glow and fog pouring out. We want and expect a demonic gateway to be something complicated and intentionally created by the most evil of people with twitchy eyes, black teeth and an old pickaxe. What we don't fully realize is that almost anything can be and it's remarkably easy to invite demons into your life. A lot of us do it daily unintentionally.

Demons need a way in. They don't just pick random people willy-nilly. They're always around looking for an opportunity but until you open the gate, they're stuck waiting on the outside. Unfortunately, gateways are easy to come by. Once in, they can make you physically and mentally sick, prideful, hateful, arrogant, lustful, the list goes on. Until then, they're waiting and watching like vultures soaring overhead. Waiting for us to turn against God. Waiting for us to break the law of God. Waiting for us to stumble or get lazy in our spirituality. Our weakness in faith and spirit is their dinner bell and they never miss a meal. They need us to turn away from God so the doorway is left unguarded. Once the way is open, even by a crack, they can establish a foothold on your life and start to take over.

Paul writes in Ephesians 4:26-27 *"In your anger do not sin. Do not let the sun go down while you are still angry, and do not give the devil a foothold."*

The word foothold in this passage should run shivers up your spine. Webster's defines foothold as, "A position usable as a base for further advance." The Free

Dictionary by Farlex further defines it in a military sense as, "An area in hostile territory that has been captured and is held awaiting further troops and supplies." When we give Satan a foothold in our lives, he establishes a base in which to operate. From there, he pushes the door open more and demons come flooding in. If the foothold is strong enough, they'll take over by the thousands.

Interestingly enough, it's fascinating to me now how we sometimes like to joke about demons and trivialize their existence when we blame them for letting us overeat or shop too much. We name sports teams and cars and even insecticide after them. They've somehow managed to get on the "What's Cool" list. We package demons in the same manner that we do Leprechauns or Gremlins. Satan doesn't mind. It keeps us off guard. But demons are real. Evil is real.

Grammy award winning recording artist Lady Gaga, spoke insightfully about the influence of evil by saying, *"Please do not forget, that hatred or evil, or whatever it is you want to call it, it's intelligent. It's smart. And it's invisible. It's an invisible snake, that while it is planning to make its attack, it is thinking to its self, 'I am going to divide my enemy into smaller, less strong groups.*

And then I'm going to make them hate each other, so that it's easier to take them down.' And as we're all yelling at each other trying to figure out which group it is that's causing the problem, evil is winning."

So many things in our lives that have the potential to drive us away from God, are constantly pulling at us; pornography, drug use, alcohol, music, movies, and advertisements, even the news – the list is endless. The Demons can't enter a person without a way in but they can occupy dwellings and objects. They sit and they wait. They have all the time in the world. For a lot of us, their job is easy. Carrying your cross through daily life is a life and death struggle. Never forget, a war is going on for your soul. The fight is dirty and full of prison rules. Satan doesn't take sick days or holidays and will devour you in a heartbeat if you allow it. Sadly, most of us allow it. If demons can use something as simple and addicting as your phone or a video game to pull you away from God, they'll use it.

The Fly in the Master Bathroom

Can rooms be possible gateways? Absolutely. It's widely believed by religious and non-religious alike that gateways or portals not only can be rooms, but doorways, mirrors and basements. Mirrors, in particular, have long been associated with paranormal activity. Victorian spiritualists believed mirrors allowed spirits to freely travel back and forth and always covered mirrors when someone was about to die for fear that their spirit would become trapped inside. Some exorcists even expanded on this and believed if they could trick a demon into looking at itself in a mirror, it would become trapped and the mirror could then be broken thus banishing the troublesome demon.

Starting in the fall of 2015, we had a fly that always hung around the sink area of the master bathroom. It's just a fly, so what? Right? I thought that too. Our master bathroom doesn't have a door. The doorway into the bathroom is rather wide and why the house wasn't built with a door to the master bathroom I'll never know. Directly on the opposite wall from the sinks, there's a doorway to a very deep walk-in closet and next to that is large Jacuzzi tub with a rather large framed mirror on the wall beside it. The fly was never in any other part of the house. Just right there in the sink area of the master bathroom.

Every day I killed the fly. Every next day, there appeared a new fly that only hung around the master bathroom. As the seasons changed and the weather got colder and the snows fell, the appearance of the fly never changed. Every day I killed it. Every day, there came a new one. Just one. Not several flies that I had to chase around. There was always, only one. One. Big. Black. Fly. This lasted throughout the winter when it was much too cold for flies. We never saw any outside. Not any in the garage by the trash. Not a single one in the kitchen where you'd expect them to be buzzing between the windows and the blinds. The fly could have easily flown around the house at any time, bothering us in several different rooms of its choosing. But it never did. It stayed in the sink area of our master bathroom.

Sure, by it self, it could be considered at worst an oddity – probably nothing to grab Holy water for. Things in nature have explanations. Fair enough. One night during this time in January 2016, Aiden decided he was going to sleep in Amanda's bed and mine with us. We always let the kids do this when they wanted to. We figured there would come a day when they'd be too old and too big and we'd look back on those days when we'd get woken up with elbows and knees in our backs and fondly miss them. So in between us Aiden slept that night. During the night he awakened to a sound coming from the master bathroom. Now remember, there's no door, just a wide doorway. What he awakened to terrified him. He said he saw a large black figure emerge from the darkness into the doorway that stood almost ceiling high with a head that he described as being crocodile. He hid beneath the sheets, closed his eyes and prayed for Jesus to protect him. When he peered out from the sheets again, the figure was gone. The next day, there was another big black fly in the sink area of the master bathroom.

Four Little Demons

I had a lot of gateways. Mine were mostly intentional. My demons had a legal right to enter my life and wreck whatever chaos they desired, because not only did I allow it, I welcomed it as well. Now of course I didn't plan on them wrecking the place like Marilyn Manson in a Poughkeepsie, NY hotel. I expected them to watch over my family and me. I assumed they would. Instead of Rottweiler's, I had them. We live and we learn.

A gateway of mine came in the form of a cute demonic kid's toy. The gateways don't always have to be obvious, dark and brooding. In fact I dare to say that most are probably innocent looking. We can open one up and never think twice about it then later wonder why our lives are chaotic.

A very good friend, who incidentally, was the Shaman that brought me into Wicca so many years ago, sent me four demon themed toys for Christmas. That's probably the weirdest sentence I've ever written. Despite being demonic in style, they were actually cute and didn't look scary at all. They were soft and brightly colored and one was red and black and charmingly named after Satan. I kept that one in my studio. He was mine. The others I gave to the boys to play with. I didn't think anything of it and was thankful for the nice gesture.

Immediately after receiving the toys, Amanda and the boys got very sick and it lasted an entire month. I was the only one unaffected. Right about this time was when Aiden was seeing monsters, I was traveling frequently and Amanda had just started talking to Monica about things that were going on. We had the toys a few months and my only concern was to hide the Satan one that sat in my studio when my parents came to visit. I didn't need the questions nor did I want the drama. A perfect storm was brewing and we unknowingly had gateways opened up all over the place.

I've known this friend for years and I know he had no ill intentions on sending us the cute demonic toys nor do I think he put a hex on them. I'm sure he didn't think anything bad since he was the one that actually designed them. With that said, shortly after Father Ray came to visit, Aiden was terrified one night by 3 monsters that he said were lurking in his closet. As with most demonic issues that went on and plagued my family, I was in Chicago away from it all. He sat on his bed staring at the closet describing them as one being brown and two being black. According to Amanda, he was clearly scared. She got into mama bear mode and approached the closet. When she opened the door, it broke off the track and seized up rendering it unusable. She wedged her way in to find only a large plastic toy bucket. She fished through it briefly and found the 3 brightly colored demon toys buried toward the bottom.

By now, Amanda had seen enough to start putting things together and she scooped up the toys from the closet, snagged the one in my office, put them into a bag and tossed them out the back door for Father Ray to retrieve and dispose of. He had already incinerated several things for us like Wiccan and Enochian books, as well as pentacles. In fact my custom made satanic ring is now blessed and sitting at the bottom of the Kansas River, courtesy of none other than Father Ray.

To Amanda's fading surprise, the monsters that haunted Aiden's closet were gone. That very next morning he said he couldn't see them anymore. Life seemed good again. She called me in Chicago and told me all that had happened and reminded me to take a look at the closet door in hopes that I could repair it when I returned. She said she tried and couldn't make it budge. Like force opening a welded jar of pickles, this had "Manly Job" written all over it. I assured her I'd handle the problem.

When I returned from my trip, I went upstairs into Aiden's room and to my surprise, saw that the door to the closet was fixed and working perfectly. Nothing looked or felt broken. I moved it. I opened it. I closed it. I opened it again. It worked just fine. I yelled down to my wife that I was proud of her for figuring out the door and fixing it. There was a long pause. Then she asked, "It's working?" I said yes and in a partly confused partly worried voice she said, "I haven't touched it and the boys haven't either."

Satan comes to you as a friend – as a cuddly toy – as a song, a movie, a web site, a sport, a job, a promotion, a car, as money, as anything that will make you let your guard down. In 2 Corinthians 11:14 Paul writes, *"But I am not surprised! Even Satan disguises himself as an angel of light."* He can work his way into your life while at the same time making you think he doesn't even exist. Peter writes in 1 Peter 5:8, *"Be alert! Watch out for your great enemy, the devil. He prowls around like a roaring lion, looking for someone to devour."* He doesn't use the word "pester" or "annoy" or even "nibble". Peter warns us that Satan is looking for someone to "devour".

There is a quote by Tucker Max that goes, *"Satan doesn't come dressed in a red cape and pointy horns. He comes as everything you've ever wished for."* Stay vigilant and stay alert. Pay attention to what brings you closer to God and weed out what pulls you further away. Don't be devoured.

6

Legion

"My name is Legion, because there are many of us inside this man." –Mark 5:9

In June of 2016, I planned one of my trips to Chicago and started the normal prep routine, which included Amanda withdrawing money from the bank so I'd have cash in case I needed it. I always ended up needing it. About $30 of it always went toward a Chicago style pizza the instant I got into town. So when she returned from doing errands and withdrawing money, I expected a normal conversation and report about it without any surprises. However, it started off with her looking at me wide-eyed and smiling and saying, "Don't be mad, I gave half your traveling money away to a homeless guy."

I think I laughed to keep from being mad. Did I hear that right? Half of my travel money? To whom again? I shook my head and kept laughing to hold back the irritation. I had to travel with that money. Suddenly I was down half of it and needed to keep an extra eye on how I used it on my trip. The irritation was beginning to win the battle when Amanda said, "But listen, it was the weirdest thing. God told me to do it." My irritation subsided and was replaced with instant curiosity. Then she started to tell me the story of why I had half of my travel money.

She had gone to the bank first and withdrew my travel cash while it was fresh on her mind. She didn't want to get busy with other things and forget since I was heading out that next morning. She had several places on her "to do" list. Bank, Target and AT&T store was at the top. Bank was done, money in hand, on to the next place. After Target was completed, she pulled out and started to get on the highway when she saw a homeless man standing on the side of the road with a sign.

This wasn't the first person she'd ever seen standing by the road with a sign. Like most other people, she often just tried to avoid eye contact. If you don't see their eyes, you can pretend you didn't notice them. It lessens the guilt. Society has trained us to be overly cautious with our charity. How many people holding signs on the side of the road are really legit? How many of them will buy alcohol or drugs or even fold up their sign and walk a block or two down the road and get into the BMW and head home when they get tired of panhandling? We quickly justify ignoring them and they're forgotten about almost as fast as we pass them.

But this encounter for Amanda was very different. As she passed the man, she had a voice in her head that told her to give the man $100. She shook it off. How ludicrous. We aren't made of money. That was half my travel cash. I relied on that. She shook it off again and continued down the road, but the voice came again, "Give that man $100". She laughed at the voice and still tried to suppress it and push it down and out of her mind. She drove faster away and again the voice told her, "Give that man $100." The voice wouldn't leave her alone. The more she tried to logically justify not doing it, the more the voice told her to do it. By now she was miles away from the man she saw and the voice was constant. She pulled over and turned the car around and headed back to where she saw him.

When she saw him, she pulled up, rolled down her window and motioned for the man to come over. She handed him the $100 and told him, "I was told to give you this." The homeless man thanked her as he took it and he walked away. Amanda was unsure what to make of the encounter. Plus we were now down $100. Her thoughts were interrupted by a tap on her window by the man she had just given half my travel money to. She rolled down her window and he said, "Go home and read Mark 5." He said nothing else. He smiled at her and walked away. She describes him as being very recognizable – someone you could easily pick out of a crowd. She's never seen him again since then.

Of all things he could have said, he said that. Of all the chapters and books and storied in the bible, he told her specifically Mark 5 – a chapter that focuses heavily on demons. The very thing we were dealing with at home. He told her as if he knew our situation.

In Mark chapter 5, Jesus and his disciples travel by boat to the region of Gerasenes, which was on the eastern side of the Sea of Galilee. The Sea of Galilee is a somewhat large freshwater lake in Israel approximately 13 miles long and 8 miles wide. They had spent the previous day on the opposite side where a large crowd had gathered to hear Jesus teach from a docked boat while everyone remained on shore (Mark 4:1). Later that evening as we read in Mark 4:35, Jesus tells the disciples, "Let's cross to the other side of the lake."

"When Jesus climbed out of the boat, a man possessed by an evil spirit came out from a cemetery to meet him. This man lived among the burial caves and could no longer be restrained, even with a chain. Whenever he was put into chains and shackles – as he often was – he snapped the chains from his wrists and smashed the shackles. No one was strong enough to subdue him. Day and night he wandered among the burial caves and in the hills, howling and cutting himself with sharp stones." – Mark 5:1-5

From a distance he recognized Jesus and ran to them bowing low and shrieking in verse 7, *"Why are You interfering with me, Jesus, Son of the Most High God?"* Let that swirl around in your head. Demons know Jesus. While many people during this time were trying to get a grasp on exactly who this Jesus was, the spirits that dwelled within this man knew very well who he was as they address him as "Son of the Most High God." There was no question. They didn't need to feel him out to be sure it was in fact Him. They knew. They trembled before him and feared his presence. Like cockroaches when you shine a light will scatter, so will demons when faced with the light of God.

When Jesus asks the man's name in verse 9, he replies, *"My name is Legion, because there are many of us inside this man."* Now stop and think about that word for a moment. Legion. What images flash in your mind? In Roman times, a Legion was the largest unit of the Roman army numbering over 5,000 men. And not just any men, mind you, but the Roman's elite heavy infantry. These were trained killers guilty of countless atrocities. Much like the demons that are all around us, and like the demons I had in me.

The legion possessing the man in the cemetery spots Jesus before he ever makes it to shore as read in Mark 5:6, *"When Jesus was still some distance away, the man saw Him, ran to meet Him, and bowed low before Him."* The reverence here is astounding. They didn't sit back and wait for Jesus to come to them. These chain snapping demons ran their host out from the cemetery where he had been living to meet Jesus when he steps out of the boat and they throw themselves down before him and beg for his mercy. Not one demon, but thousands of them as evident by their incredible physical strength. Picture over 5,000 of some of the fiercest soldiers Satan has to offer bowing low at the feet of Jesus and you will picture the magnitude of this meeting.

The man that Amanda met told her to go read Mark 5. By this time I had surely allowed evil spirits by the thousands to invade our home. They controlled our lives and certainly controlled me. They wrecked havoc on my family and tormented us to the point that we felt very isolated much like the man living in the cemetery. The only one that could drive them away was Jesus and this stranger that Amanda went back to find, knew it. I believe God sends us angels, and the person you try to ignore tomorrow may very well be one.

7

The Chicago Prayer

"Therefore I tell you, whatever you ask for in prayer,
believe that you have received it, and it will be yours."

–Mark 11:24

Father Ray made several visits to our house with
his team and I slowly started opening up more and more. I
started to not mind their visits. I felt betrayed by Satan
and I wasn't happy about it. I feel silly to admit that I was
upset about that. Like being upset that the rattlesnake you
were holding bit you. It makes sense when you step back
and see it with fresh eyes but your vision is tunneled
when you're holding the snake. Even still, I had a hard
time letting go and still lived in a state of denial.

Amanda started RCIA (Rite of Christian Initiation
of Adults) with a parish that was 45 minutes away. I had
no interest in that. Even with all I had seen and
experienced, I wasn't ready to embrace the Catholic life.

My demons still had a hold on me and I held on to the feelings that they were still family. We all have disagreements and may even argue with family at some point but we normally don't up and abandon them. No blood no foul – water under the bridge. But the problems persisted and my demons weren't happy in the least.

Amanda learned that things wouldn't ever get better with our family until I finally surrendered my life to God and entered the church. That didn't fill her with hope. As the man of our family, I was the spiritual leader of our household and therefore set the pace for the spirituality and tranquility of our home, or the lack of it. I didn't want that job. It felt the equivalent of someone asking me to teach advanced biophysics to Harvard graduate students. Thanks but no thanks. I was a fraud, how could I ever be qualified to be a spiritual leader? Amanda and the boys needed me, and I felt hopeless watching them being tormented and toyed with as I struggled unsuccessfully to smooth things over with Satan. My denial had a death grip on me and I couldn't come to terms with what was happening. I spiritually shut down. My demons took full advantage. I could often times feel them around me and the hair on my arms would stand straight up. I'd spin around and flip them off and shout an obscenity or two at them. If anyone heard or saw me, they'd surely think I was losing my mind. Meanwhile, Amanda continued on with RCIA and I continued to not support it.

The Prayer

My trips to Chicago would last anywhere from 1-2 weeks just depending on what was going on. This particular trip lasted 2. They were always hard on Amanda and the kids but they understood and they knew I loved my work. But while I was away, the spiritual warfare would always increase dramatically. It never failed. I went on a trip and the rest of the family went to battle. I always heard about the struggles and always felt there was nothing I could do to help. I couldn't fix anything. The problem was too big for me and I assumed it was too big for God. I was still thinking like a Satanist.

Prayer for me was always somewhat of a mystery. I hated it when I was following Satan and referred to it as "begging". But even long before I turned to the evil one, prayer and the idea behind it tended to elude me. Why pray for something when God already knows the outcome? I'm sure people have debated this for hundreds of years if not longer. The idea behind it building a relationship with God wasn't anywhere in my thought process.

In James 5:16 we read, *"Confess your sins to each other and pray for each other so that you may be healed. The earnest prayer of a righteous person has great power and produces wonderful results."*

Paul puts it simply when he writes in 1 Thessalonians 5:17, *"Never stop praying."*

Never stop. Don't just pray when you need things. Don't just pray when someone else needs things. Don't just pray when you're in trouble or sick or struggling or happy, sad, troubled, hungry, tired, or in need of guidance. Never stop praying. Some translations say, *"Pray without ceasing."* Any good relationship needs communication. We too often treat God like a Walmart Superstore. We only go to him when we need something and only if it's convenient to get there.

On day 8 of my 2-week trip, Amanda was mentally drained. Her lack of sleep combined with the stress of dealing with spiritual attack left her in a state of helpless depression. The kids were acting out because they too were tired and had little sleep. This of course just made things worse. We spoke on the phone and she was getting ready for another sleepless night and hoped she'd get at least 2 hours. She said she wasn't holding her breath for that but hoped anyway. My heart sank. I wanted to be there.

I hung up and sat for several minutes quietly reflecting and soaking everything in. I had taken up room and board in my friend's semi-finished basement for the length of my stay. It was late, and it was quiet. I just sat and thought. I sat and listened. I opened myself up and listened for God's voice. For the first time in my life, I had a seeking heart. David writes about this in Psalms 63:1, *"In my heart, I long for you, as I would long for a stream in a scorching desert."* I was in the desert and I ached for that stream. I needed God.

I smiled and thought it would be really nice and convenient if the coffee table would suddenly burst into flames and God's booming voice would resonate out of it. But God comes to you in a whisper as written in 1 Kings 19:11, *"Go out and stand before Me on the mountain," the Lord told him. And as Elijah stood there, the Lord passed by, and a mighty windstorm hit the mountain. It was such a terrible blast that the rocks were torn loose, but the Lord was not in the wind. After the wind there was an earthquake, but the Lord was not in the earthquake. And after the earthquake there was a fire, but the Lord was not in the fire. And after the fire there was the sound of a gentle whisper. When Elijah heard it, he wrapped his face in his cloak and went out and stood at the entrance of the cave."*

I heard the whisper. I felt an unquenchable need to talk to God in prayer. Getting up from my chair, I walked into the bathroom that was close by, closed the door and knelt down next to the bathtub. The fact I was in a bathroom didn't bother me. I needed a private place for this conversation and this was the most private room in the house. I had never before kneeled in prayer. I opened my heart to God acknowledging all I had done up to that moment and my lack of faith and trust and everything else just came out and I laid it up on the altar. I then prayed for my family and pleaded with God to protect them and watch over them. I knew he would. I had no doubt in my mind that what I was asking would not go unheard. I felt it. I then ended my prayer and went to bed.

The next morning I called Amanda eager to find out how their night went. She sounded happy. She sounded rested. There was excitement in her voice when she told me they all had slept wonderfully and the entire night was peaceful. I think that was the moment when my heart finally turned. It was my "Ah hah moment." God heard me. God didn't ignore me after all I had done to reject him. He was there for me and I felt loved. I felt his presence. I felt protected in ways that weren't on Satan's menu.

In 2015 actor Denzel Washington delivered a commencement address at Dillard University in New Orleans. In the address, he told the graduates to "Put God first." In talking about God, he said, "I didn't always stick with him, but he always stuck with me." Deuteronomy 31:6, tells us, *"Be strong and courageous. Do not be afraid and do not panic before them. For the Lord your God will personally go ahead of you. He will neither fail you nor abandon you."*

I told Amanda about the prayer I had done and she was as encouraged and mind blown as I was. I spent the remaining nights of my trip, on my knees in the bathroom of my friend's semi-finished basement, praying.

8

Fall Down Seven Times,
Stand Up Eight

"Yet what we suffer now is nothing compared to the glory He will reveal to us later." –Romans 8:18

It would be nice to end the book right here and tell you that everything went smoothly from there on out. That I was free of my shackles and Satan packed up and moved on. Unfortunately, Satan doesn't give up that easily. Thankfully, God doesn't either.

With all difficult struggles, there are victories and setbacks. Satan wasn't about to let me go and I had moments when I didn't want him to. He was my security blanket. He was my spiritual woobie. I was scared of letting that go and feeling naked, vulnerable, and alone. I had constant thoughts that no one would accept me and I'd be outcast and that my real place was back in Satan's care. I was loaded with doubt and wasn't anywhere ready or willing to be the spiritual leader my family needed.

Amanda marched forward with RCIA with Monica by her side. I attended a few Protestant churches in the area but I had the same frame of mind that I had the last time I attended church. My heart wasn't there and I had one foot out the door. I was back in my noncommittal comfort zone where I "played church" and tried to chalk that up as changing my life. God knows when his children aren't doing what they're supposed to do. He always knows. Just ask Jonah *(Jonah 1-4)*.

Amanda mentioned that in order for her to move forward, we had to get our previous marriages annulled. After months of purposefully dragging my feet, I finally gave in and contacted my ex wife and got the process started. I wasn't happy about it but I knew that this Catholic stuff Amanda was doing was important to her. So I thought what the heck. I'll do it for her. If that will make things better at home then sure, sign me up. I still didn't like it though. It felt odd going back into the world of my ex wife. It felt even more odd telling her that I needed info from her so that the Catholic Church could render our marriage invalid. No part of that was fun. But she agreed. I think she wanted me out of her life as badly as I did and if this would do it then so be it. I was glad to be done with Catholic issues.

Shortly before Easter, we got word from the Parish that Amanda was attending that they had lost all her paperwork regarding the annulment. It was gone. I don't think it fully hit Amanda until we were sitting through Easter Vigil Mass and she had to watch her RCIA class enter the church without her. She was devastated, discouraged and angry. She let Satan have a foothold and I encouraged her to give up on her Catholic pursuits. She fell away feeling defeated. But there is one thing I learned about Amanda. She might fall down. She may even get knocked down. But she'll get back up. There is a Japanese proverb that reads, "Nana korobi ya oki" which literally means, "Seven falls, eight getting up" or modernly worded, "Fall down seven times, stand up eight." That's my wife. It didn't take her long to bounce back.

While she was bouncing back, I was losing more and more interest. I had confided in a few people at the local Protestant church I was attending about my Satanic past and struggles and it seemed the few I told couldn't back away from me fast enough. I think one of them actually stepped back a couple feet as if to make room for the lightening bolt that was surely coming. I'm sure not everyone would have reacted that way but I wasn't willing to find out. I felt like a leper and thought Satan was right. I wouldn't be accepted. I would be outcast. I lost hope. I got knocked down pretty hard and I didn't feel like standing.

I'm not sure when Amanda started planting blessed Sacramentals on me. She saw my discouragement and I think feared I would completely give up. Her fears we well justified. I felt myself spiraling. If you're sitting there wondering what I'm talking about, you're probably not alone. I didn't know what Sacramentals were for a long time either. Basically, Sacramentals are blessed objects that point us toward God. A more detailed description would explain them as, "sacred signs, which bear a resemblance to the sacraments. They signify effects, particularly of a spiritual nature, which are obtained through the intercession of the Church. By them, men are disposed to receive the chief effect of the sacraments, and various occasions in life are rendered holy" (Catechism of the Catholic Church, No. 1667).

The Sacramentals that most people are used to seeing are Holy Water, the Crucifix and the Rosary. Not to be confused with "Sacraments" of which there are 7 and they are Marriage, Eucharist, Baptism, Reconciliation, Confirmation, Holy Orders and Anointing of the Sick. Osv.com does a great job describing Sacramentals in more detail. The ones that Amanda planted under my mattress, in my car, in my jacket, in my coat, in my dresser, and probably numerous other places that she may have forgotten about, were small medals that depicted the Archangel Michael and Saint Benedict as well as some that had images of Mary. I didn't know until later, that blessed objects always surrounded me thanks to my tenacious wife. I may have been ready to throw in the towel but Amanda wasn't. She's a scrapper. Satan was about to find that out.

My mom always said something to me which when I was younger, I just blew it off as silly religious nonsense. She would say, "Kaylan, there are no such thing as coincidences." This was always followed by an eye-roll from me. It wouldn't be until decades later when I would finally understand what she meant and pass it along to my own kids.

Amanda started getting strong thoughts and urges to attend Mass but wasn't really sure where to go. Monica had told her about a certain Parish that was located about 30 minutes away from us about a year prior but Amanda never tried it out. According to Monica, they had a 5:00 teen Mass every Sunday evening that featured amazing music and an upbeat atmosphere without sacrificing the reverence of a traditional Mass. Coincidentally, Amanda found herself close to the church at around 4:45 while out shopping for groceries and other things we needed to get us through another week. Her hair was in a ponytail, the knees of her jeans were ripped out but she felt as though she was being pulled there regardless. I can hear my mom's voice in my head already. Let me rephrase my earlier statement. Amanda didn't find herself close by the church coincidentally, but by the grace of God, Amanda found herself near the church just in time to pop in for Mass to see what it was like. Sheesh mom.

Amanda liked the service so much that she came home and told me about it and was shocked to not hear me groan and shut her out. In fact, it was quite the opposite. I agreed to go check it out with her the following Sunday. I had never heard of a Mass with cool Protestant style music. I had assumed they were all sit, stand, kneel confusing workouts for a solid hour that felt every bit like five. But she said it was fun and energetic and the message was great and the time flew by. This, I had to see. I was skeptical to say the least.

I'm a musician. I have been one since I was 6 years old playing air guitar on my Granny's wooden-handled breadboard. There was a time when I almost failed out of college because all I wanted was to make it big with the band I had at the time. My dream was to wake up, stagger out of the tour bus in whatever town I had forgotten we were in, run sound check at the venue and cash my royalty checks. It's funny how plans always seem to change.

Once the musicians hit that first note as Mass started, my ears perked up. It was good. I was really good. It was so good I wanted to be over there playing along side them. It set the pace for how the rest of the evening went. I didn't have a lot of Masses under my belt to really compare to but it wasn't horribly confusing and boring like I had convinced myself it would be. It was fun. I didn't know what was going on but it was fun none-the-less. Amanda was surprised to hear my enthusiasm after it was over. In fact, we were both surprised. I liked it. I wanted to go again. So the following Sunday evening at 5:00, we went again. I liked that one too. My demons had enough and they were fed up. Trouble was coming – serving size large.

The Sundays that followed were rough. That's really putting it lightly and void of the 4-letter words I'd like to add to that description. Our house was combative. Both Aiden and I stalked the house like short-tempered bulls looking to pick a fight with anyone over anything. Just getting out of the house to get to Mass was a battle. Every Saturday evening I felt sick. If I wasn't sick, one of the boys was sick. We'd feel the buildup by Saturday and by Sunday all Hell broke loose – so to speak. You could feel the spiritual tension hang in the air and coat your lungs like coal dust as you breathed it in. It felt just as toxic. When we'd return home from Mass, I'd have to lie down and sleep for 2-3 hours even though I wasn't tired a mere hour before. The harder we fought to make it to Mass, the worse the battle seemed to be. After the service ended, we'd find one of the priests standing out in the foyer and ask for a blessing for the entire family. That always seemed to help.

After our fourth Mass we were talking with Father Allen out in the foyer after receiving our weekly, much needed blessing. He mentioned that they offered RCIA classes year-round. I surprised Amanda again by quickly agreeing to it. I had seen enough. I was angry with Satan and he had made it personal. So I doubled down and the fight was on. We had started going to Mass in May and by June we were about to start RCIA as a family. I was sticking it to the man. Booya! Later that week, while walking through my studio, I felt the hair on my arms stand straight up as it always did when I felt the demons lurking nearby. My temper got the best of me and I whirled around, gave the finger to whatever dark spirit was in the room with me and snarled, "Bring it." Well bring it they did and it was war.

Paul writes in Ephesians 6:10-12, *"A final word: Be strong in the Lord and in His mighty power. Put on all of God's armor so that you will be able to stand firm against all strategies of the devil. For we are not fighting against flesh-and-blood enemies, but against evil rulers and authorities of the unseen world, against mighty powers in this dark world, and against evil spirits in the heavenly world."*

The enemy has us surrounded and they are armed and ready. How armed and ready are we as a society?

How armed and ready are you? Satan and his armies work tirelessly to take us down. Like doomed Serengeti antelope trying to cross a crocodile infested river, so too are the poorly equipped, the uninformed and those that choose to reject God. The enemy lies in wait and will show no mercy. You will be pulled beneath the current as quickly as you enter it. We aren't talking about a lone-wolf demon that pokes at you to over eat – the one whose only ambition is to end up as a decal on the side of your hot rod. We're talking about legions, battalions, and thousands upon thousands of what Paul describes as evil rulers, authorities, mighty powers and evil spirits. Their only job is to destroy you.

That first Sunday in June, we walked into Mass with intentions of attending our very first ever RCIA class as a family. This was huge and I was a mess. I couldn't see. My vision was doubled. I couldn't focus on anything during the service. My eyes hurt. I couldn't hear. Everything sounded like babble and broken gibberish. It was just noise and I couldn't make sense of anything. I felt nauseous. I had stimulation overload and I needed out. I needed out immediately. So I got up, maneuvered my way out of the pew and left my family sitting there puzzled. I didn't even look back. The distance to the door felt like a mile.

Amanda found me a short time later when they were dismissed to attend RCIA classes. I told her what had happened and after we took a few minutes, we slowly made our way to where the classes were scheduled. I didn't fare well there either. I didn't want to be there. I quickly regretted my bold decision to take this road. I didn't have the armor for this God stuff. I doubted everything I was doing and everything I had done to put me in an RCIA class. How in the world did I let myself get into a Catholic Bible class? My trust in God was failing and I was getting pulled beneath the current to be devoured.

In Matthew 14:25, Jesus walks on water toward the disciple's boat at about 3am. After the disciples get over their expected and rational fear, Jesus calls out to them to not be afraid. Then in verses 28-31 we read, "Then Peter called to Him, 'Lord if it's really You, tell me to come to You, walking on the water.' 'Yes come,' Jesus said. So Peter went over to the side of the boat and walked on the water toward Jesus. But when he saw the strong wind and the waves, he was terrified and began to sink. 'Save me Lord!' he shouted. Jesus immediately reached out and grabbed him. 'You have so little faith,' Jesus said. 'Why did you doubt me?"

Even Peter, the rock on which Jesus built his church, had doubts about where he was and what he was doing. His trust in Jesus faltered and as a result he started to fall beneath the waves. In a panic, he was wise enough to reach out for help from the Lord and in turn Jesus was right there for him. I needed to reach out for Jesus. I needed to reach out to the one who proved to be there when others weren't. I was sinking so I reached out and Jesus grabbed my hand.

A short time later, in the very early stages of RCIA in 2016, during a meeting at our home with a couple of Father Ray's team members, I finally broke down and revealed the fullness of my satanic involvement. I had kept it secret for too long and I admitted to the depth of my convictions toward Satanism, including the pacts I had made. Amanda was very stunned of course but suddenly a lot of dots connected for her. Everything made sense at that moment and she and I knew war was indeed coming.

9

War

"Then there was war in heaven. Michael and his angels fought against the dragon and his angels. And the dragon lost the battle, and he and his angels were forced out of heaven. This great dragon – the ancient spirit called the devil, or Satan, the one deceiving the whole world – was thrown down to the earth with all his angels."

–Revelation 12:7-9

War had been declared in the James household. There was a clear power struggle going on and it was messy. Battle lines had been drawn and sides had been picked. And as scared and uncertain as I was at times, the side I picked wasn't with Satan. We were officially on the outs.

We wasted no time and decided that we'd get the boys their own crucifix to hang by their beds. We already had a few around the house and wanted to be sure the kids were covered as well. After purchasing them, we had them blessed. We were arming ourselves with righteousness as well as Sacramentals. Each stand very well on their own, and when combined strike a heavy blow to the armies of Satan.

"A woman in the crowd had suffered for twelve years with constant bleeding, and she could find no cure. Coming up behind Jesus, she touched the fringe of his robe. Immediately, the bleeding stopped. "Who touched Me?" Jesus asked. Everyone denied it, and Peter said, "Master, this whole crowd is pressing up against you." But Jesus said, "Someone deliberately touched Me, for I felt the healing power go out from Me." When the woman realized that she could not stay hidden, she began to tremble and fell to her knees in front of Him. The whole crowd heard her explain why she had touched Him and that she had been immediately healed. "Daughter," He said to her, "your faith has made you well. Go in peace." – Luke 8:43-48

The woman in this story reached out and touched the fringe of his robe. She didn't grab a handful of it nor did she put her hands all over it. She managed to reach through the crowd and get possibly a few fingers on the edge of his garment. Notice too that she didn't touch his hand, his arm, or any physical part of Jesus. She only touched a physical tangible object that was blessed merely by being worn by Jesus. Her faith in him as well as her faith in the blessed garment he wore allowed her to be healed. Like this woman in the crowd, we too wanted healing and had faith that God would watch over us and heal us, and in the same token, we had faith in the blessings bestowed upon the Sacramentals that we hung by the kid's beds.

About an hour later, we had the boys in bed and Amanda and I were lying on our bed watching a show together. The night had gone quietly for the most part. Nothing crazy. No wrestling with the boys or with the dog. No mock silly Taekwondo battles in the kitchen with Amanda in full Karate Kid sweep the leg style. There was nothing out of the ordinary. It was a pretty boring night, and it felt wonderful. But that soon changed.

As we were lying there, I felt heat on the back of my neck. It came on suddenly and it was uncomfortable enough for me to notice. I reached back and felt raised lines on my skin – long ones. They hurt at the touch and my confusion peaked. I reached over and clicked on the light and asked Amanda if there was anything on my neck.

"Uuuuummm yeah," she said. "You have 3 deep scratches back there. What on earth did you do?"

I told her I hadn't done anything and that I'd just been lying there and suddenly felt it. She grabbed her phone and took pictures so I could see them. Sure enough, it looked like 3 claw marks about an inch apart, one on top of the other. They were thin, as though made with something very sharp and the skin was red and raised up quite a bit. Had I done that myself, I would have noticed when it happened. No, this was sinister in nature and shots had been fired.

I'd never before been hit by a demon – at least not that I ever recalled. I know back when I proudly followed Satan, I had wished to have an encounter with one in the same manner I wished to have an encounter with a bear when I was a Wiccan. Now that it had actually happened, I wasn't all that happy about it. Apparently purchasing, blessing, and hanging crucifixes was enough to bring retaliation. It seemed surreal being marked by something in the spirit realm. At first I wasn't all that sure how to feel about it. I think it instantly solidified a lot of things for me and changed my attitude. A lot of uncertainties became certain. Demons were real. The spirit world was real. The

Demons in the house were upset and whatever relationship I thought I once had with them was now obliterated. Fine. Soon afterward, I went and purchased a statue of Mary and had that blessed for the house. They could choke on that.

Unfortunately, Aiden became our spiritual attack barometer. We could tell how good or bad things were based on how Aiden was. He was an easy target and they went after him often – cowards. We fought them tooth and nail and Aiden was always hit hardest. Incidentally, Padre Pio has always been his favorite Saint and has been known to have physical altercations with demons. Aiden wanted to be a saint like Pio. He was a trooper despite the attacks. I wanted to trade places with him. It should have been me, not my child. I felt he was paying for my disloyalty and I often wanted to quit just to keep him safe. But I knew that was Satan whispering in my ear and the only way to keep Aiden safe was to keep fighting. So we struggled forward and took the devil head on.

Holy water blessings became a nightly ritual and we always knew when the battle was bad when Aiden refused the blessing and didn't want to hear any prayers. When asked why, he would say through tears that they hurt. So Amanda would hold him in her arms and I'd say the prayers anyway over the sounds of the screaming. Sometimes he would writhe in his bed as though he was in pain. By the time the prayers were over, he was often calmed down. I felt so guilty for bringing the armies of Hell into my home. It was my fault. My ignorance and arrogance allowed my family to be owned as much as I. We got knocked down, but we kept getting back up.

An RCIA sponsor told me about a retreat coming up. I immediately didn't want to go. Thereafter, anytime I saw them, they mentioned the retreat. I smiled each time it was brought up and responded with, "Yeah sounds good, we'll see." I had no intention of going but I ended up signing up for the retreat. No, actually let me take that back. Amanda signed me up for the retreat. I was officially on the God train and I was still dragging my feet. This was uncharted territory. I wasn't comfortable at all with spending all day at a Catholic retreat. I could think of a million things I wanted to do instead. To top it off, it was going to start early on Saturday. Besides I wasn't Catholic enough yet for a Catholic retreat. I didn't know enough. In the week leading up to it, I tried to think of every excuse not to go. I know that sounds odd, considering the situation we were in. But Satan is crafty. If he can't derail you directly, then he'll do it indirectly.

Even Moses himself doubted his ability to do as the Lord wanted. In Exodus 4, God instructed Moses to return to Egypt and convince the Pharaoh to free the Jewish slaves. Moses replies in verse 10, *"But Moses pleaded with the Lord, "Oh Lord, I'm not very good with words. I never have been, and I'm not now, even though You have spoken to me. I get tongue-tied, and my words get tangled."* Then, a few moments later in verse 13, Moses is still looking to avoid what God wants of him. *"But Moses again pleaded, "Lord, please! Send anyone else."* We know that Moses did in fact do as he was asked and we know the miraculous events that followed. For anyone that doesn't know the story, I won't give away the ending. Go check it out. It's a good one.

Just a few days before the retreat, Amanda got really sick. She was bedridden and I really wasn't sure if I was going to be able to attend the retreat at all. It was out of my hands – void of responsibility. Perfect! But Amanda insisted I go and my sponsor was going to attend as well. It was as if God saw that coming. It's interesting to side note how many times one of us would get sick during times of observations, services, holidays or activities that were religious in nature. It was every time. It never failed.

Now Amanda had been in bed for days with Flu symptoms. She hadn't done any sort of extraneous activity. No playing with the dog, the kids or even me. While I was attending the retreat, which lasted the entire day, she felt what seemed like long hair strands on her back. She kept reaching to get them, but couldn't. When I returned home, she asked me to look at her back. Upon looking, however, they weren't hair strands. Covering her back were 9 long thin scratches made by something sharp. The skin was red and raised around them and they covered her as though she had been whipped. The same looking marks as the ones I had on my neck. She had been demon hit. The war waged on.

On a Monday night in December in 2016, I received a call from Dave, who was one of our RCIA sponsor team members. We had amassed a team round us by this time and everyone had a specific much-needed role. Dave informed me that he had gotten with Father Ray and they were coming out to the house that coming Wednesday and I'd be doing my formal Renouncing. I froze. I had climbed to the top of the high dive over the last several years, made my way to the very edge and didn't want to jump.

For the remainder of that night, I was in a panic. Wednesday night was coming. It was in the books and going down. Despite all the attacks, the scary events, and the frequently occurring bouts of despair that filled our house, I didn't want to let go. You don't leave your family. I kept thinking that over and over. We had an argument. After we calm down things will be okay. I rationalized everything I could to not shut that door to my life. I didn't want to leave.

I remember when I was 5-years old; I was going to run away. I had been told no about something and that was it. I had enough. I was done and declared that I was running away and heading out for greener pastures. My parents agreed that there were probably more fun places that would just let me do what ever I wanted and said they were sad to see me go. They helped me pack and made me a sandwich and walked with me to the door and bid me good luck. I confidentially stomped out the door, got to the end of the driveway and took a left down the sidewalk. I got about halfway past the yard and stopped. I didn't take another step. I didn't want to leave after all. I experienced the same feeling 41-years later when I hung up the phone with Dave.

I was an emotional wreck. Renouncing felt so final. Through all the spiritual growth and reflection, I was still tethered to my past. In my mind, I was still a Satanist even if the identity was buried deep beneath the surface. I had doubts that I could actually leave Satan. I paced the house. I was filled with fear that I'd be stuck in some sort of void where God's Church wouldn't accept me and Satan wouldn't either. I feared I'd be spiritually homeless. I feared everything. I had put up a good fight and stomped out the door with my sandwich. But now I just wanted to run back and make amends. God was ready for that. Again, he sent an angel. He sent Amanda.

She sat with me on our bed and tried to help me pray. I couldn't focus very well on anything she was saying. I couldn't read the prayers that she put in front of me. I could hardly repeat along with the ones she said aloud. I felt sick trying to pray and just as sick trying to hear it. I felt nauseated.

I somehow managed to make it through a Hail Mary prayer and heard distinctly over my right shoulder just outside the door, an audible disgusted throaty hiss.

For you Tolkien fans, think Gollum. The boys were asleep in their beds and I know their sounds very well. It wasn't them. I asked Amanda if she had heard the same thing I did. She said she hadn't and I described it for her. I had felt the demons and now I had heard them. I wasn't a big fan of either but I didn't want to leave it all behind. It was the world I had grown accustomed to. It was the world I knew. It was also the world I was about to renounce in just two days.

The following day was better. I had a feeling of calm wash over me, and the anxiety and fear I had subsided. My mind felt clearer and was able to regain some focus. The battle from the night before was tough and I felt I had lost a lot of ground. I let the enemy take over areas that I assumed to be secure. I had basically let my guard down and felt overrun. The devil is a cunning adversary. But with God's help, he can be defeated.

"But resist him, firm in your faith, knowing that the same experiences of suffering are being accomplished by your brethren who are in the world. And the God of all grace, who called you to his eternal glory in Christ, after you have suffered a little while, will himself restore you and

make you strong, firm and steadfast. To Him be the power for ever and ever. Amen." –1 Peter 5:9-11

10

Cutting the Ties

"So he returned home to his father. And while he was still a long way off, his father saw him coming. Filled with love and compassion, he ran to his son, embraced him, and kissed him. His son said to him, 'Father, I have sinned against both heaven and you, and I am no longer worthy of being called your son."

"But his father said to the servants, "Quick! Bring the finest robe in the house and put it on him. Get a ring for his finger and sandals for his feet. And kill the calf we have been fattening. We must celebrate with a feast, for this son of mine was dead and has now returned to life. He was lost, but now he is found.' So the party began." –Luke 15:20-24

The calm lasted until about 30 minutes before the team was to arrive for the renouncing. I felt my confidence slipping but held it together. God set things in motion and there was no stopping it. I felt all I could do was just hold on.

I knew for quite a while that the renouncing would eventually one day come. I had assumed that I'd just have to renounce 1 thing, 3 at most. After meeting with our sponsor team and talking one night, it was discovered that it was in fact 9 things that I'd be cutting my ties to. We ended up making a list. Incidentally, it was during this meeting that I mentioned my Wiccan name being Jael. Remember telling you to remember that name? Come to find out, Jael, also known as Jehoel, Jehuel, Jaoel, and Jah-el is the guardian angel of presence and chief of the order of seraphim. He brings a stillness and clarity of mind as well as peace into your life. Ancient Jewish writings talk of Jael being the one keeping the Leviathan in his prison. Through all those years resisting God, I had an angel with me all along from the start. God always has a plan.

The team really didn't waste any time. Father Ray led the pack and got right down to business. I was torn. I couldn't decide if I was happy to end my pact with Satan or run out the door and hide until they left. Even at this stage in the game I was apprehensive. This was it. I was going to officially announce to Satan and his army that I was no longer theirs. I bounced back and forth emotionally. I still had fears of letting go. Hell was working hard to keep me and I was filled with doubt.

Just a couple years prior, Father Ray stormed through my home and my life like Sherman's March through Georgia. I recalled how much I loathed him and his team. I recounted how my skin crawled during his prayers and the horrible things that went through my mind. How since that first day, I've learned to not only love and respect them but rely on them as well. And now I sat and watched him once again put on his vestments and prepare things for my renouncement of all my satanic ties. I once again felt a feeling of peace and knew I was on the right path. I took a deep breath and remembered how many times Jesus instructed to not be afraid. That peaceful feeling, however, was going to get wrestled from me.

I had nine different things to renounce and had to read quite a bit for each one of them. I couldn't just batch renounce. Each item on my list had special attention. We weren't doing an express lane cleanse. They were thorough. They were prepared and as we got started, I felt the hair on my arms stand straight up. I knew things were lurking about. I could feel them.

I started reading. I started off fine and read quicker than normal; partially to just get through with it and partially because I didn't want Satan's goon squad to tamper with the process. That was just wishful thinking. I should have known better.

By the time I started to renounce my pact with Satan, my focus on the words I was reading became blurred. The words on the page seemed jumbled. I had already read them a few times for other things on my list, but now I found myself struggling and had to follow along with my finger and make out each world as I came to it as though I'd never laid eyes on them before. I stuttered. I couldn't hold the book I was reciting from steady. My hands shook. My body shook. That's when I noticed how incredibly cold it got in my house. Another person on the team with me that night felt it as well.

I marched forward slowly. There was no turning back now. My demons hated me and I was letting them know that the feeling was mutual. I was moving on, moving out. Leaving behind my management spot in Hell and all the perks that came with it, even though I knew by then, even the promise of perks was a flat out lie.

I began to renounce my contract with the demon I had loved as much as Lucifer and that's when the words on the page no longer looked like words. It all looked alien and I didn't recognize a single word. I started to cough and couldn't stop. The air got colder for me and the coughing continued. I shivered harder and was no longer able to focus on the renouncing. I couldn't hold the book any longer and handed it back over. Father Ray told one of the team members to get a glass and fill it with Holy Water. A few moments later, they returned with the glass and I was instructed to drink it all. After doing so, I sat the empty glass down and was able to read the words and finish without a single cough. Even the house felt warmer and I was no longer shaking. It was done.

Days after my renouncing, we learned that it was held on the last day in the liturgical Holy Year of Mercy. Dioceseofraleigh.org describes it well by saying, "*Traditionally, every 25 years the Pope proclaims a holy year, which features special celebrations and pilgrimages, strong calls for conversion and repentance, and the offer of special opportunities to experience God's grace through the*

sacraments, especially confession. Extraordinary holy years,
like the Holy Year of Mercy, are less frequent, but offer the
same opportunities for spiritual growth."

The feeling of not being tethered to a past that I felt defined me was indescribable. Before that night, no matter what I did or how many Masses I attended, I still felt like a Satanist because I didn't have the courage on my own to stand up to Satan and officially say "No more!" I often felt guilty for even thinking of leaving and the feelings wouldn't stop until I gave in and continued on with the charade. Until I continued on with the lies I had burned into my mind. My past was too unforgivable. My story would scare people off. I'm forever marked so I may as well stay with those that understand and welcome me and while I'm at it I may as well indulge myself in life's pleasures. After all it was God that made them, why not partake in them? And mostly, my problems and my sins are too big even for God.

I didn't have to think that way anymore. I was free of that lie. I felt free of the shackles that Satan kept me in. I was able to look back with wiser eyes and forward with clearer ones. God kept his promise. He never left me.

"Fear not, for I am with you; be not dismayed, for I am your God; I will strengthen you, I will help you, I will uphold you with my righteous right hand." –Isaiah 41:10

I felt loved when I returned to God. I felt accepted. I felt strengthened. I felt overwhelmed with joy and scared to death at the same time. I felt like I was floating. I had burned my security blanket and there was work to do. But first, I had to let go of the wheel and let God drive.

11

Letting Go of the Wheel

Trust in the Lord with all your heart, and do not lean on your own understanding. –Proverbs 3:5

So now everything was smooth sailing. The fog and darkness lifted, I turned away from Satan, opened my heart and my life to God and was free of all temptation and spiritual attack. Life was perfect. Right? Well... not so much. In fact, it wasn't even close. Life wasn't instantly bliss after I renounced and severed my path with Satan. I had a lot of hang-ups – a lot of spiritual baggage. I still do sometimes. You don't go through decades of something and turn it off as easily as turning off a light. The difference is that I'm aware of it now. Sure I still fall in the swamp but at least I'm aware that I'm waist deep in it. Then, with God's help, I can change course and try to do better. But even changing course is sometimes easier said than done. Satan is always there, looking to get a foothold.

The spiritual attacks didn't stop either. I was just a bigger target and a nicer trophy. Only this time, I stepped out onto the battlefield armed with God and ready. But even with all the armor, the weapons and the increasing knowledge, I still fall short, as we all tend to do. But now we're better prepared for the fight. Now we feel like the Disney/Pixar movie characters from "The Incredibles." Bring it.

For me, the "eye for an eye" rule was a hard one to let go of. I wasn't a big fan of forgiveness. If you look around at the world today, it's definitely something we all have a hard time with. In Matthew 5:38-39 Jesus says, *"You have heard the law that says the punishment must match the injury: 'An eye for an eye, and a tooth for a tooth.' But I say, do not resist an evil person! If someone slaps you on one cheek, offer the other cheek also."*

Satanists have a much different idea about that. According to the Satanic Bible, I was taught to "Hate your enemies with a whole heart." How many of us are guilty of that and don't recognize it as coming from Satanist teachings? We repackage it and resell it as something acceptable like being a good patriot or belonging to a certain political party and hating those that don't agree.

God teaches us to love our enemies. *"But to you who are listening I say: Love your enemies, do good to those who hate you, bless those who curse you, pray for those who mistreat you." –Luke 6: 27-28*

Satanists twist the verse in Matthew 5 it into something that I carried with me and to this day have a hard time with from time to time. The teaching is, "And if a man smite you on one cheek, smash him on the other! Smite him hip and thigh, for self-preservation is the highest law!" The actual rule as stated in the Eleven Satanic Rules of the Earth reads, "When walking in open territory, bother no one. If someone bothers you, ask him to stop. If he does not stop, destroy him."

My seven year old complained once of a girl from school that was being mean to him. This happens, they're seven. Kids are still learning social skills at that age. Filters are still being developed. At that age, being unkind could mean that you like that person. It's all so confusing. I had the perfect opportunity to sit him down and mentor him like a good father should. But, I immediately went to my eye-for-an-eye closet and told him to next time tell her, to the shock of my wife, "Well you're just a rotten hag and you'll end up alone and barren with a house full of cats." Parent fail. Christian fail. Fails across the board.

Mind you, this is after my renouncing. Not years before. I wanted this little girl to pay dearly for hurting my son's feelings. Smash them on the other. No mercy. My response was overkill to a 7-year-old's problem. Even to an adult situation it was too much. Our desire to dish out punishment when we feel wronged is off the charts and it comes from one source and it isn't God. Can you imagine what this world would be like if we all stopped and realized that those thoughts and actions were satanic in nature? How many arguments would be settled peacefully? How many conflicts would end? How many bad situations could be completely avoided? We want to dish out angry justice when our pizza is made wrong or when someone takes our parking space and yet Jesus hung on a cross with huge iron nails driven through his hands and feet. He had blood running down his face and most likely into his eyes from the beating and the thorns driven into his head and yet as he was dying he forgave those that put him there.

We react in such ways because we either have zero trust in God or we have very little. We don't trust that God is in control and therefore we step up and take on the role of judge, jury and executioner. We don't trust that God will take care of things as we see fit and to our liking. We don't trust that God will take care of things on our schedule and our deadlines. We don't trust that God is even watching or even worse, caring.

While they're getting better, I still have trust issues. Trusting in God is hard. We constantly try to drive the boat. We like driving the boat. Driving the boat makes us feel productive, empowered, ambitious, or a number of other good feelings that give us validation. We want to be in control all the time and daily life tells us that we CAN be in control and should be. We have self-help books, self-help classes, self-help web sites, seminars, small groups, videos and even memes. We have an abundance of self-help and it's always interesting how very little of that tells us to turn to God and let Him help and let Him guide us. We might briefly turn to God when things go bad, but then we push him aside and hop right back into the drivers seat.

In Daniel 6, Daniel is serving in the Persian Empire as an administrator for King Darius the Mede. *"The king also chose Daniel and two other administrators to supervise the high officers and protect the king's interests." Daniel 6:2*

He was good at his job. So good in fact that the other administrators and officers looked for ways to get rid of him. But when they couldn't find anything to accuse him of, they created a scenario in which a law was made that forbade anyone from praying to anyone divine or human other than King Darius for a period of 30 days. Violators of the law would be thrown into a den of lions to be ripped apart. Daniel had a good relationship with God. His prayer life was spot on as written in verse 10, *"But when Daniel learned that the law had been signed, he went home and knelt down as usual in his upstairs room, with its windows open toward Jerusalem. He prayed three times a day, just as he had always done, giving thanks to God."*

So much can be said about verse 10. Daniel knew the law and the consequences of breaking it. He could have easily given up praying for 1 month. He could have lain low, and kept silent and played things safe. He could have even prayed to King Darius as the law suggests as a sign of loyalty and respect to possibly gain some extra favor with the King and have it work to his advantage. He was literally risking his life to follow God and when the time came for him to lay low, he went home and prayed for God's help.

Of course when news of this reached Darius, the king was troubled. The law was signed as an official law of the Medes and Persians that couldn't be revoked. As much as he liked Daniel, Darius was painted into a corner. He had been manipulated and there was nothing he could do but follow the law that he had signed. He had Daniel arrested and put into a lion's den and the entrance was covered with a stone and sealed.

The following morning the King went to the sealed den and called out in verse 20, *"...Daniel, servant of the living God! Was your God, whom you serve so faithfully, able to rescue you from the lions?"* Daniel answered, *"Long live the king! My God sent his angel to shut the lion's mouths so that they would not hurt me, for I have been found innocent in His sight. And I have not wronged you, Your Majesty."*

Earlier in Daniel 3:1 we read, *"King Nebuchadnezzar made a gold statue ninety feet tall and nine feet wide and set it up on the plain of Dura in the province of Babylon."* Word was sent out to "people of all races and nations and languages" as written in verses 4-5, that upon hearing the sounds of the horn, flute, zither, lyre, harp, pipes, and other musical instruments, they were to bow down and worship the statue that Nebuchadnezzar made. Those that didn't bow were to be thrown into a blazing furnace. However, three Jews, Shadrach, Meshach and Abednego refused to bow, which of course angered the king and he had them brought before him.

When they were brought before the king, they were questioned and given a second opportunity to bow before the gold statue and avoid a terrible and certain death. Again, they refused which we read in Daniel 3:16-17, "*Shadrach, Meshach and Abednego replied, 'O Nebuchadnezzar, we do not need to defend ourselves before you. If we are thrown into the blazing furnace, the God whom we serve is able to save us. He will rescue us from your power, Your Majesty.*"

Not only did this anger Nebuchadnezzar, verse 19 describes him as being so furious that his face distorted with rage. He ordered the furnace to be heated 7 times its normal temperature and had the strongest men in his army to bind them. As they were thrown into the furnace, it was so hot that the flames killed the soldiers that got too close. As Nebuchadnezzar watched the 3 men in the flames, he was astonished to see not 3 but 4 figures. He got as close as he could to the furnace and shouted to them to come out and when they stepped from the furnace, verse 27 tells us *"...the fire had not touched them. Not a hair on their heads had been singed, and their clothing was not scorched. They didn't even smell like smoke!"*

Shadrach, Meshach, Abednego and Daniel all had complete faith and trust in God. Against huge odds and terrible consequences, their trust in God was unwavering. They trusted that God would be there for them. They trusted that God had a plan and was in control. They all let go of the wheel. They were all in, even when given chances to change their courses, take control of the situation and play it safe. They trusted in God's plan, not theirs. Too often we try to take control away from God only to be devoured by lions or consumed by flames.

Notice too, how interesting those references are – lions and flames, which have been used to describe Satan and Hell among other things. Earlier in chapter 4 we spoke about the verse in 1 Peter 5:8 that reads, *"Be alert! Watch out for your great enemy, the devil. He prowls around like a roaring lion, looking for someone to devour."*

In Matthew 13:49-50, Jesus says, *"That is the way it will be at the end of the world. The angels will come and separate the wicked people from the righteous, throwing the wicked into the fiery furnace where there will be weeping and gnashing of teeth."*

Once Daniel was freed, the wicked conspirators were separated and gathered up along with their families and thrown into the den where the lions tore them apart before they ever hit the floor. The fiery furnace killed Nebuchadnezzar's soldiers, who were separated out and chosen as being the strongest, while the three faithful men were safe among the flames.

These four endured trials that many if not most would have failed. Rather than cave in and let Satan have a foothold, they stood their ground and trusted in the Lord and were victorious. So much so that those that witnessed it rejoiced in the Lord as well. They knew that God was in control, and they moved over and faithfully, unquestionably let him drive the boat.

Life doesn't suddenly turn easy when you decide to follow God. Jesus says in Luke 9:23, *"Whoever wants to be my disciple must deny themselves and take up their cross daily and follow me."* It's not an easy task and it shouldn't be taken lightly. He doesn't say take up your cross just once and you're good to go. He says daily. Not once a week. Daily. Crosses are big. Crosses are heavy. Carrying a cross is a struggle. Jesus describes it this way for a reason. The suffering Jesus went through while carrying his cross to Galgotha was brutal. You will go through hardships and may suffer for your faith. Choosing to follow God is a lifelong commitment but we often treat it like getting a gym membership. We get jazzed about doing it and then a month later the excitement is gone and we're trying to justify why we can't. God knows when you're fully committed and when you're just going through the motions. He knows when you're carrying your cross and when you're just pretending to. *"I know all the things you do, that you are neither hot nor cold. I wish that you were one or the other! But since you are like lukewarm water, neither hot nor cold, I will spit you out of my mouth!" – Revelation 3:15-16*

Letting go of the wheel signifies your willingness to do whatever task God has in store for you. You are saying, "I'm here God. Do with me as you will." And when you step up and allow God to take over, then you'd better hold on tight because you will do things you never thought you would or could. But through it all, God will be there. He'll stay by your side through every step. He tells us over and over that he won't abandon us. It's we that abandon Him. The road may be difficult and long but if you have trust in God, he'll see you through as he has done for so many before you.

12

Holy Week

The angel said to the women, "Do not be afraid, for I know that you are looking for Jesus, who was crucified. He is not here; he has risen, just as he said. Come and see the place where he lay." –Matthew 28:5-6

For those of us going through RCIA as well as Christians around the world as a whole, Holy Week is a pretty big deal. It signifies and relives the last supper, the arrest of Jesus, the crucifixion and the resurrection on the days they occurred starting on Holy Thursday, then Good Friday, followed by Easter Vigil, which is Saturday evening, and finally Easter Sunday. It is that Easter Vigil when most people looking to enter the Catholic Church become baptized, confirmed and receive the Eucharist for the first time. It had been a very long road for us and finally we were preparing to enter the church as a family on March 29, 2018. Of course it wouldn't be us without strange and amazing occurrences that continuously showed us that we were on the right road.

Lazarus

While this happened just prior to Holy Week, it is worth mentioning to go under the category of possibly strange but definitely amazing. During the second to last Sunday Mass before Easter, I stood with my family and our RCIA sponsors as Deacon John stepped up to deliver the reading of the Gospel. During a Mass, it's customary for the Gospel to be read by the Deacon present if there is one. If not, the priest reads the Gospel. Since Deacon John was present, he stepped up. As always, I hadn't looked at any of the readings before hand and once again let them just be a surprise. That never bothered me. I like surprises, as long as they're good ones. My sponsor Gordon, however, always looked at the readings before hand. He's on top of a lot of things that I'd normally not even think about. He's former military, always prepared, so it makes sense. But that day he hadn't read them either. Certainly wasn't a normal thing for him to forget. So we both stood there waiting for our surprise and God delivered one – a big one.

Deacon John began to read the story of Lazarus and I immediately turned to look at Gordon and his eyes grew as wide as mine. He had been on this journey with me and walked with me on the writing of this book. When the story of Lazarus was being read to us with less than two weeks before Easter Vigil, Gordon and I were hit with the biggest God moment. The years of struggle, the years of torment and doubt, the years of clashing with Satan and his armies all collided in that single moment while we listened to the Gospel. We stood there in awe. It was surreal, beautiful and we felt the presence of God.

Reconciliation

For weeks the idea of doing my first reconciliation loomed on the horizon. I'm sure I'm not the first to admit that I really wasn't looking forward to it. I had a lot to talk about. For anyone unsure of what reconciliation is, it's confession. As a Satanist I called it "The sorry box". I'm sure a lot of non-Satanists call it that as well. Despite the preconceived ideas of what it is and the jokes the uninformed have about it, it's actually a wonderful Sacrament that despite it's daunting and uncomfortable nature, makes you feel happy, relieved and closer to Jesus.

Now of course Jesus already knows about your sins but voicing them out loud to someone really makes you look within yourself and makes you genuinely repent for those wrong doings.

I had heard about how wonderful and free and liberating the experience would be. I heard all that and more and yet I still didn't want to do it. I felt ashamed and embarrassed and was convinced that no one in the world was more unworthy than I was to receive any forgiveness. The evil one is good at making you feel worthless. But, I did it. I survived. And the rumors are true. It does make you feel a lot better.

It was revealed to me that my first Reconciliation happened on the feast day of St. Joseph, the patron saint of fathers. Years ago when I was against Catholicism and clutching onto Satan, Amanda did a novena to St. Joseph in hopes to convert me. Novena comes from "novem" which is the Latin word for nine. So a novena is basically 9 days of prayer. So how astonishing it is, years later, I would surrender to God, and have my Reconciliation on the feast day of none other than St. Joseph that Amanda prayed would intercede on my journey.

There are no coincidences. My mother's words come floating into my head quite often now. This is a shameless plug to always listen to your mother. God doesn't accommodate to your schedule or your box or your meme or your ideas, beliefs or standards. God is all-powerful and if you think you or your problems are bigger than He, you might be on the wrong side of the battlefield. Stop and take a look at whom you're following.

The Washing of Feet

The Sunday before Holy Week, my family and I were asked if we'd like to have our feet washed on Holy Thursday. Before I go into explaining this, just know that just being invited to do this is a huge honor. There are cradle Catholics that have never experienced this and may very well never.

The washing of feet comes from the scriptures where on the night of the last supper, Jesus washes the feet of the disciples. Starting in John 13:1, the Gospel says, *"Before the Passover celebration, Jesus knew that His hour had come to leave this world and return to His father. He had loved His disciples during His ministry on earth, and now He loved them to the very end. It was time for supper,* and the devil had already prompted Judas, son of Simon Iscariot, to betray Jesus. Jesus knew that the Father had given Him authority over everything and that He had come from God and would return to God. So He got up from the table, took off His robe, wrapped a towel around His waist, and poured water into a basin. Then He began to wash the disciples' feet, drying them with the towel He had around him."

Skipping ahead a bit we read, "After washing their feet, He put on his robe again and sat down and asked, 'Do you understand what I was doing? You call me 'Teacher' and 'Lord,' and you are right, because that's what I am. And since I, your Lord and Teacher, have washed your feet, you ought to wash each other's feet. I have given you an example to follow. Do as I have done to you." –John 13:12-15

The washing of feet is a sign of servitude and humility. By washing the feet of his disciples, Jesus was in turn teaching them to be servants to others as well.

Twelve of us were invited to participate in this beautiful ceremonious act – twelve people for the twelve disciples. Amanda, Ryan, Aiden and I were chosen to be four of them and were the only ones chosen out of the

RCIA. I felt honored yet wanted to cancel. I wasn't completely sure what to think. The congregation was going to watch me get my feet washed. It was hard to wrap my mind around the idea.

The evening of Holy Thursday Mass, they called forward the twelve invited and we sat in chairs that had been placed up front that faced the rest of the congregation. We sat down and started to remove one shoe. We were told previously to only remove one shoe but I was nervous. I removed both.

I waited anxiously, eagerly wondering what the experience would be like. I had nothing to compare it to. Finally, Father Brian knelt in front of me with a basin that I placed my foot into. He took a pitcher of Holy Water from an assistant beside him and then looked up at me, smiled and whispered, "We put ice in this." That was just the bit of humor I needed and I felt at ease.

I sat with my family on Holy Thursday in front of a Catholic congregation of hundreds. Both shoes were off even though only one foot was being washed. As Father Brian poured the water over my foot and began to dry it with a towel, I instantly reflected back on everything that had happened to us since that first night in 2013. All the victories, all the set backs, all the tears and pain and doubt and learning all rushed in at once as I watched a priest kneel down and carefully wash my foot. Mine. I felt humbled and incredibly unworthy. The one who tricked a Christian jeweler into creating a Satanic ring, the one who purposefully set out to hurt faiths, the one who swore a blood oath to Satan with actual blood, the one who God never turned away from even though I fought against him for so long. My feelings of unworthiness turned into feelings of being loved. I felt I had returned home and after God embraced me, he was calling for a celebration. I had felt dead for so long and in that moment, I felt alive again.

Entering the Church

Almost five years since our journey started and nearly 2 years since we walked into our first RCIA class as a family, we had finally made it and were about to enter the church as a family. The destination that seemed a million miles away and at times impossible to reach was finally here. I felt I had reached the top of the hill, my face grimy and bruised, my hands cut, my knuckles bloody, and captured the flag at last. As I stood on my victory hill and looked back at the scared landscape from the battles we fought, I knew in my heart I had more hills to conquer. I'd never take my armor off and I'd never lay my sword down. I was now a soldier for God. And my work wouldn't be done until I stood in the presence of the Lord and heard the words, "Well done, my good and faithful servant." (Matthew 25:23)

The evening of the Easter Vigil is difficult to describe without spoiling it for anyone wanting to go through it at some point. The best way I can think to describe it would be, heavenly. There is so much reverence displayed for what is taking place. It's not a quick dunk followed by two measures of a hymn, and a sprint to your car. This is a celebration that makes you feel that the angels themselves are all in attendance.

Amanda was baptized and that was wonderful to witness. She had been looking forward to that for so long and finally seeing it felt surreal. I was then called up and stood in front of the congregation and made a profession of faith. That too, was surreal. Following my profession of faith, myself, along with the rest of the family and others in attendance entering the Church that evening, received Confirmation. I was never quite sure what that was before starting RCIA. According to USCCB.org (United States Conference of Catholic Bishops), *"Confirmation deepens our baptismal life that calls us to be missionary witnesses of Jesus Christ in our families, neighborhoods, society, and the world. We receive the message of faith in a deeper and more intensive manner with great emphasis given to the person of Jesus Christ, who asked the Father to give the Holy Spirit to the Church for building up the community in loving service."*

After we were Confirmed, we received the Eucharist. I could write a book just on this topic alone and there are already many of them out there. For Catholics, the Eucharist IS the body and blood of Christ. *"As they were eating, Jesus took some bread and blessed it. Then he broke it in pieces and gave it to the disciples, saying, 'Take this and eat it, for this is My body.' And He took a cup of wine and gave thanks to God for it. He gave it to them and said, 'Each of you drink from it, for this is my blood, which confirms the covenant between God and His people. It is poured out as a sacrifice to forgive the sins of the many."* – *Matthew 26:26-28*

As I stated before, I was raised around Protestant communion growing up. I felt that I was actually receiving it for the first time on Easter Vigil. It was different. Every single Mass centers on the Eucharist and you can receive it every single day of the year. It's an amazing Sacrament that puts your heart, mind and soul in the right place when you take up your cross daily and follow God.

I stepped up and ate the bread and drank the wine and went back to my seat and kneeled in prayer. I felt like a new person – a new man. I now had on a full set of armor. The Holy Spirit had descended upon us all and I was ready to go into battle for God against the very ones I'd clung so hard to for so long. I had to have a seeking heart, and once I did, God was there. *"Keep on asking, and you will receive what you ask for. Keep on seeking, and you will find. Keep on knocking, and the door will be opened to you. For everyone who asks, receives. Everyone who seeks, finds. And to everyone who knocks, the door will be opened."* –Matthew7:7-8

The struggle is real. A lot of us walk around in a daze and we can't figure out why bad things happen and why life is, at times, so chaotic. We point to everything we can think of and never point to the source. Many don't even think Satan exists and those that do don't take him seriously enough. They don't fathom the influence he has and therefore never realize the noose around their necks until they're dangling from it unable to breathe. This is Satan's domain. This is where he fights. This is where he works. We're merely visitors and without God in our lives, we're outgunned and outmanned. You're at war whether you care to believe it or not and only through God will you get the armor and weapons to survive it.

Glorify God in all that you do and let others see Him working in your life. God took a dedicated proud Satanist and turned him into his disciple. When I died spiritually, God was there. He never left. Just as Jesus told Mary and Martha that Lazarus' situation happened by the Glory of God so that the Son of God would receive glory from it, so too did he know that I'd be alright as well and He would receive the glory. He called me from my tomb and I came out. God can do all things because he always, always has a plan.

13

Helpful Prayers

Then you will call on me and come and pray to me,
and I will listen to you. –Jeremiah 29:12

I've listed a number of prayers that have helped my
family and I along our journey and still do. They're taken
from several different sources and they've done us
extremely well. There are many more out there that may
be better suited for your particular situation. No matter if
you use these, find others or pray on your own, approach
the Lord with a seeking heart and He will always listen. I
promise.

Our Father
Our Father,
who art in heaven,
hallowed be Thy name;
Thy kingdom come;

Thy will be done on earth as it is in heaven.

Give us this day our daily bread;

and forgive us our trespasses

as we forgive those who trespass against us;

and lead us not into temptation,

but deliver us from evil. Amen.

Hail Mary

Hail Mary, full of grace. The Lord is with thee.

Blessed art thou amongst women,

and blessed is the fruit of thy womb, Jesus.

Holy Mary, Mother of God,

pray for us sinners,

now and at the hour of our death. Amen.

Glory Be

Glory be to the Father,

and to the Son,

and to the Holy Spirit,

as it was in the beginning,

is now, and ever shall be,

world without end. Amen.

Saint Michael Prayer

Saint Michael, the Archangel, defend us in battle.

Be our protection against the wickedness and snares of
the devil.

May God rebuke him, we humbly pray;

and do thou, O Prince of the heavenly host,

by the power of God

cast into hell Satan and all the evil spirits

who prowl throughout the world seeking the ruin of souls.

Amen.

Guardian Angel Prayer

Angel of God,

my Guardian dear,

to whom God's love commits me here,

ever this day (or night) be at my side,

to light and guard, to rule and guide. Amen.

Binding Evil Spirits

In the name of the Lord Jesus Christ of Nazareth, I stand
with the power of the Lord God Almighty to bind Satan
and all his evil spirits, demonic forces, satanic powers,
principalities, along with all kings and princes of terrors,

from the air, water, fire, ground, netherworld, and the evil forces of nature.

I take authority over all demonic assignments and functions of destruction sent against me, and I expose all demonic forces as weakened, defeated enemies of Jesus Christ. I stand with the power of the Lord God Almighty to bind all enemies of Christ present together, all demonic entities under their one and highest authority, and I command these spirits into the abyss to never again return.

I arise today with the power of the Lord God Almighty to call forth the heavenly host, the holy angels of God, to surround and protect, and cleanse with God's holy light all areas vacated by the forces of evil. I ask the Holy Spirit to permeate my mind, heart, body, soul and spirit, creating a hunger and thirst for God's holy Word, and to fill me with the life and love of my Lord, Jesus Christ. Amen.

Denouncing the Occult

Heavenly Father, in the name of your only begotten Son, Jesus Christ, I denounce Satan and all his works, all forms of witchcraft, the use of divination, the practice of sorcery, dealing with mediums, channeling with spirit guides, the Ouija board, astrology, Reiki, hypnosis, automatic writing, horoscopes, numerology, all types of fortune telling, palm readings, levitation, and anything else associated with the occult or Satan. I denounce and forsake my involvement in all of them in the name of Jesus Christ who came in the flesh, and by the power of his cross, his blood and his resurrection, I break their hold over my life.

I confess all these sins before you and ask you to cleanse and forgive me. I forgive myself and ask you Lord Jesus to enter my heart and create in me the kind of person you have intended me to be. I ask you to send forth the gifts of your Holy Spirit to baptize me, just as you baptized your disciples on the day of Pentecost.

I thank you heavenly Father for strengthening my inner spirit with the power of your Holy Spirit, so that Christ may dwell in my heart. Through faith, rooted and grounded in love, may I be able to comprehend with all the saints, the breadth, length, height and depth of Christ's love, which surpasses all understanding. Amen.

Anima Christi

Soul of Christ, make me holy

Body of Christ, be my salvation

Blood of Christ, let me drink your wine

Water flowing from the side of Christ, wash me clean

Passion of Christ, strengthen me

Kind Jesus, hear my prayer

Hide me within your wounds

And keep me close to you

Defend me from the evil enemy

And call me at the hour of my death

To the fellowship of your saints

That I might sing your praise with them

For all eternity. Amen.

14105719R00077

Made in the USA
Lexington, KY
04 November 2018